Los Angeles Music Center   *Gilbert Emerson Moore*

Mixed Media on Masonite   *48" x 48"*

THE HIGHER ORDER OF SCIENCE

Harmony of Being

by

IRENE S. MOORE, C.S.
Author of *The Bridge* and *Identity*

DeVorss & Co.—Marina del Rey, California

Printed in the United States of America by
STOCKTON TRADE PRESS, INC.
Norwalk, California 90650

ABOUT THE AUTHOR

Born in New York City, Mrs. Moore was educated in local schools. Her first Christian Science membership was in *Eighth Church,* New York City, where she was a member of various committees. Subsequently moving to Connecticut, she transferred her membership to the Greenwich *Church of Christ, Scientist.* While there she served as Assistant Librarian, Sunday School teacher, Church Treasurer, and member of the Executive Board. She had class instruction with an authorized teacher in 1950 and became listed in *The Christian Science Journal* as a practitioner in 1955. Soon after this Mrs. Moore moved to California and transferred her church membership to *Twenty-Eighth Church* in Los Angeles. She served on several committees here also. She was chairman of the Lecture Committee prior to writing her book, *The Bridge.* Because of its publication she was excommunicated from both the Christian Science church organization and her branch church in 1972. Since then she has written two volumes on *The Higher Order of Science,* the first titled *Identity,* and the present volume, *Harmony of Being.*

I dedicate this book to my family, to my husband's family and to all of my friends. They, as well as the many inspirational authors I have read through the years, have added a great deal to the harmony of my being.

ABBREVIATIONS

used in the footnotes for the writings of Mary Baker Eddy
in their final revised form (as of 1910).

Mis.   Miscellaneous Writings

My.   The First Church of Christ Scientist and Miscellany

No.   No and Yes

'01.   Message to The Mother Church, 1901

Pul.   Pulpit and Press

Ret.   Retrospection and Introspection

S. & H. Science and Health with Key to the Scriptures

Un.   Unity of Good

References to *The Holy Bible* are found in the *Authorized
King James Version*, printed by *Oxford University Press.*

INTRODUCTION

In my classes on the higher order of Science, the book, *Harmony of Being,* evolved quite naturally as part of a sequence from my previous books, *The Bridge* and *Identity*. In any discussion of this new book, I feel it is necessary first to spend a little time on the nature of the two earlier ones.

The Bridge was enthusiastically and lovingly written to describe my spiritual unfoldment out of the orthodoxy of Christian Science into its higher order, the exalted view found within the teaching. This higher order of Science within Christian Science gave positive direction to my work as a Christian Science practitioner. My consistent holding to the premise that "All is infinite Mind and its infinite manifestation, for God [Good] is All-in-all,"[1] which I have mentioned in this book, resulted in a marvelous realization of Oneness. Of course this meant renouncing the dualism of denial and affirmation, for I saw that continuing in this way would never bring the unifying concepts I was reaching for so sincerely. The answers to my questions came as I held to the higher order statements by identifying with them without reservation.

The response to *The Bridge* was very gratifying, and it was not long before I found myself preparing classes on the subject of Identity. The book that followed,

---

1. *S. & H.* 468:10-11

titled the same, was meant to inspire students to identify more personally with the higher order statements contained in Mary Baker Eddy's works and the Bible also: ". . . the kingdom of God [all substance, Spirit] is within you." In this book, *Identity,* I took the definition of God from the *Glossary* of *Science and Health with Key to the Scriptures,* and I showed how natural it is for one to accept the synonyms for God personally as one's own God-Being, and how reasonably possible it is to relate them to everyday experience.

As one applies the inspiration obtained from *The Bridge* and *Identity,* he is brought harmoniously into a full realization, discovering within himself ". . . a pure peace, a fresh joy, a clear vision of heaven here,—heaven within . . . and an awakened sense of the risen Christ."[2] He finds his celestial life acceptable to him here on earth. It is in Truth his spiritual habitation. God is known to us to be the Center and Allness of Being and, since we know that all there is to us is universal love, we are grateful for every path pointing the way to our risen Christ.

In this book, *Harmony of Being,* we praise and glorify all healing as coming from Mind, expressing itself as infinite love. In other words, having crossed our bridge, we know how to identify divinely and how to live harmoniously for we have learned the way in the higher order of Christian Science to ". . . recognize man's spiritual being . . . [to] behold and understand God's creation,—all the glories of earth and heaven and man."[3] And we do so *now.* We learn, too, that the inner enlightenment of our divine being reveals the great

2. *My.* 155:18-20
3. *S. & H.* 264:28-31

realities of Mind, God, Good, for use in our present earthly realm. Our physical structure then is understood to be one of Truth and Love in a divinely personal way, and its recognition as this creates our heaven, harmony, within us, and we see it everywhere.

Living and loving this higher order gives us a happier, more total joy, a continuing revelation of our personal divinity and an appreciative consideration for the divinity of others. The harmony of our Being moves us into stimulating experiences that relate to the wholeness of life; it gives broader concepts to all we survey. Its beauty expands into an infinite interpretation as we realize that we are living our harmonious and eternal lives now.

Irene S. Moore, C.S.
Los Angeles, California

HARMONY OF BEING

We shall not cease from exploration
And the end of all our exploring
Will be to arrive where we started
And know the place for the first time.[1]

. . . behold, the kingdom of God is within you.[2]

We are of one mind in this class today. Because of our unity we can explore together the origins of the peace and harmony within us, intently and joyously, and, with the satisfaction that follows, reach out single-heartedly into the kingdom that is already ours.

The Science of Celestial Being is our heritage. Its loving function rests in us as the Christ-consciousness, a priceless possession for which our gratitude is boundless. From it the Science of Life unfolds to us as infinite revelation. Keeping in mind (our Christ-Mind) the God-Being awareness which is centered on the fact of our divinity, we accept our prize, this Oneness, this grand discernment, this unique clarification of our material/spiritual universe. We live in the brightness of

---

1. T. S. Eliot: *Little Gidding,* Four Quartets, Published by Harcourt Brace Jovanovich, Inc., New York, N.Y.—also by Faber and Faber, Ltd., London—p. 15.
2. *St. Luke* 17:21

our divine glory today; we identify with the harmony of our being, the heavenly happiness, joy, and the bliss within us.

In our study of the higher order of Science we enjoy the thoughts of many writers in addition to those of Mary Baker Eddy, although we may be more familiar with *Science and Health with Key to the Scriptures* and *Prose Works* as sources of inspiration. We lovingly relate what we read to our present observable, divine universe which spiritual sense (Mind) informs us is so marvelously beautiful in its material sense manifestation. We express personal/spiritual love in enduring and practical ways and we find ourselves individually more responsive to a world peopled with spiritual ideas in the flesh. For the many opportunities that come to us to glorify our ever-expanding soul senses we are grateful. The higher, extended view comes to us as inner revelation. Its illumination brings a world of ideas to our attention, encouraging us to rise to an increasing awareness of our capabilities as the realm of Mind.

In *Unity of Good,* 52:4-7, we find that "This Science of God and man *is* the Holy Ghost, which reveals and sustains the unbroken and eternal harmony of both God and the universe. It *is* the kingdom of heaven, the ever-present reign of harmony, *already with us.*" (Italics mine). From the work we have done in our study of *The Bridge* and *Identity* we recognize this quotation as one which states the higher order within Christian Science, and it is with such statements that we are in accord today. Remember: We do not have to try as hard as we used to when we were in the instruction of Christian Science in order to sustain the harmony of our Being, for now it is quite obvious that this harmony cannot be closer than that which is "already with us."

I like to use the phrase "crossing our bridge" and, in this case, having moved from the dualism of orthodoxy to a Oneness premise, we are consciously identifying as our God-Self in the realm of celestial existence with our harmony established. Realizing more than we did before, we see *ourselves* as the structure of Truth and Love, having all the containment of a spiritual-material nature in a harmonious living and loving of divine completeness. Practically applied this kingdom presents to us the reward of work well done, with peace and confidence, with joy, health and holiness—an all-pervading atmosphere characterizing our spiritual habitation-at-hand.

The real purpose of our personal/spiritual exploration as the Harmony of Being is to provide ourselves with a fuller understanding of this being which we are. First of all, let us understand: We are talking about our heavenly being here in the flesh. We receive our security from the foundation of Wholeness/Oneness that exists as the very center, the nucleus of our Being. Principle, Mind, Soul, Spirit, Life, Truth and Love constitute this foundation and it is from these that we cannot be moved. Harmony is the expression of these seven synonyms for God; it comes to our everyday experience as we apply them to our lives. We are not trying to gain something by searching for it; we know *we already have* the harmony, peace and joy of our celestial being this very moment. Our way of experiencing Truth is to accept its presence within us before its evidence appears. We take the grand opportunity to express this divine withinness, this Science of Being which we are, at all times and wherever we may be regardless of circumstance or condition. We are always at the point of divine knowing, recognizing the spiritual revelation that proclaims our divine essence.

We accept the invitation, written by Mrs. Eddy, ". . . to rise higher and still higher in the individual consciousness most essential to . . . growth and usefulness; to add to . . . treasures of thought the great realities of being, which constitute mental and physical perfection."[3] Visible emergence of consciousness as the human/divine personality, and its total acceptance, advances us to these heights. *We baptise ourselves*, refreshed and strengthened in our Oneness. In the acceptance of this identity we reach Self-knowledge in the fact of our spiritual conception, past, present and future, the grand totality of our existence.

———————

Attending a symphony is indeed a joyous experience. Our soul senses receive the harmonious sounds that come to us; we give wholehearted attention to what we hear. We listen, each with his own kind of listening, individually fashioned by his divine sound-receptivity. In this light I ask you to recall some of the Association meetings or some of the lectures you attended where, at the end, you shared what you received with another listener. Sometimes you found out that what you heard was not at all what your friend had heard. Each of us in tune with his harmony of being receives a fruition specifically his own, and the more

———————

3. *'01*. 1:11-15

one knows about his true self, the greater he values the experience that comes to him. So it is with spiritual identity. In our accord today as the Science of Celestial Being we have great harmonies within us; we express them as soul senses. Do you remember identifying with this statement: "Harmony in man is as real and immortal as in music"?[4] Make it your present heritage; accept it and have it remain with you forever!

In this class I ask you to tune in naturally and joyously to the Harmony of Being as an essential part of your immortality. Let this joy *possess* you. Let our consonance extend to our families, our friends, our communities, to our government and throughout our universe. Some may ask just what I mean when I use the word "harmony." Perhaps I can define it rather formally as a concordant agreement between parts of a whole. More simply, it is a pleasing arrangement of ideas. In any event it has an infinite number of applications to our lives and in its unity of thought and action it brings a tolerant, even joyous, relationship to us all in the grand experience called Life.

Listening to the harmony within us reveals our divinity; we hear truths emerging as ourselves. Through the receptivity of Love we understand that there are varieties of tones and moods of life. Each person uses his highest understanding of them, and for this reason we do not adversely judge him. We know all senses to be divine, for all the faculties of Mind are in truth beautiful faces of Soul. Our attentive listening reveals a *new* song in our hearts, or *an amplified one* or a *more definite one*. Whichever it is, we are its fullness of joy

---

4. *S. & H.* 276:14-15

and peace, and in this divine atmosphere the words
"Harmony in man is as beautiful as in music . . ."
(*S. & H.* 304:20-21) bring an essential truth into our
being.

I must have felt this one day when I wrote the following poem:

THE SONG WITHIN

All minor chords for me this day
    Are sounds of symphonies
Filling my soul with joyous ecstasy,
    For here within I feel the peace
Of Love's sweet harmony.

All phrases of instrumental chords
    Hold me, fill me with a
Fount of praise and gratitude for
    Life's sweet cadences.
I rejoice!

Whatever thoughts I hear today,
    Whether dark or swift or low,
A song rings out its melody,
    Its sweet assurance that
All is well.

Each of us must have the feeling of possessing a
"song within." Making it your very own, you feel in
tune with your universe and you walk the glorious
avenues of your celestial existence. In the divinity of
your senses you recognize your divine being and this, in

turn, allows you to see the same divinity in others. But before you see theirs you must see your own, for we are closest to ourselves. We must recognize harmony within us to bring it into evidence in those we meet. The Russian dancer, Nureyev, remembering his childhood, recalls a ballet performance he saw which made a tremendous impression upon him, so much so that it changed his life. The important thing here is that he felt the possibility of becoming a dancer within himself before he found corroboration of it in other dancers. Let him describe this event to you:

> From that unforgettable day when I knew such rapt excitement I could think of nothing else; I was utterly possessed. From that day I can truthfully date my unwavering decision to become a ballet dancer. I felt "called." Watching the dancers that night, admiring their "out of this world" ability to defy the laws of balance and gravity, I had the absolute certitude that I had been born to dance .... From the age of about eight I can truthfully say I was possessed.[5]

Now I am not asking that we all become ballet dancers, but rather that we may be similarly possessed as the Science of Harmonious Being in whatever capacity we may be "called." We, too, may experience such an absolute certitude, the unquestioning assurance that *we are here to be Science* with all its heavenly

---

5. Rudolph Nureyev: *Nureyev, An Autobiography*. Copyright (©) 1962 by Opera Mundi. Reprinted by permission of the publishers, E. P. Dutton & Co., Inc., New York. pp 42 and 44.

attributes unique in form and substance to each one of
us.

"To reach heaven, the harmony of being, *we* must
understand the divine Principle of being."[6] This refers
to *our* being, *our* divine Principle, and although the
instruction of Christian Science has exposed us to it,
the higher order of Science *gives us the understanding*
to experience this heaven. The harmony is here in all
our undertakings without our having to dispel error by
"handling" animal magnetism because our Principle of
Being accepts no duality in Mind, no opposite to Truth
that must be overcome, no misconception to unsee.

Your presence here today shows how much you value
the harmony within you. Your divinity has brought you
here to renew your understanding of the perfection of
your spiritual natures in the flesh, embodied as you.
Enjoy this harmony, your very Christ Being, *possessed*
as you are of Life, Truth and Love. Be grateful for every
moment of your daily living. For the word "possess"
I take the definition found in Webster's dictionary:
"To maintain in a condition of control or tranquility;
as to possess one's soul in patience." Replace the word
"patience" with the word "love." Maintain yourselves
in tranquility. Possess your soul as love.

I feel that I have had an opportunity to put this
control, this tranquility and love, into harmonious action. After I had written *The Bridge,* The Board of
Directors of The Mother Church found that ". . . the
publication of such a book by a Christian Science practitioner without prior consideration . . . [is] highly unusual [and one which] requires an explanation." To

6. *S. & H.* 6:14-16 (Italics mine)

this I answered: "Yes, there is an explanation. It is a book which I have written as an exposition of the higher order of Science referred to in *Misc. Writings,* 99:12-14 ('Men and women of the nineteenth century, are you called to voice a higher order of Science? Then obey this call.') Here Mrs. Eddy asks for obedience to a higher understanding of our Science. In another reference, *Science and Health,* 367:27-29, she says, 'I long to see the consummation of my hope, namely, the student's higher attainments in this line of light.' *The Bridge* is explaining these *higher order* references and many others, bringing them into clearer focus." In maintaining my position as the higher order of my Being, I remained at peace throughout all my correspondence with The Board of Directors, and my harmony continued in all dealings with The Executive Board of my branch church as well.

Following my correspondence with The Board of Directors in Boston I had a most surprising experience one rainy day when a man representing the Committee on Publication came to my door. There had been no phone call and no letter had arrived informing me of his visit. I did not allow him to come in for I was not in the habit of seeing visitors without an appointment. I asked him to telephone me that afternoon, and I told him that I might be interested in seeing him if I knew the reason for his visit. He did call later that day but said he could not discuss over the phone why he wished to see me, so I suggested that he write to me about it. He could not do this either. Suspecting his motive in calling, I asked him if it was in any way connected with a book I had written. He preferred not to answer this either. Then I asked him if he had read

The Bridge. He said he had not, so I simply told him
I could not see him. I felt he had been sent to ad-
monish me about my book, and I certainly would not
put anyone in a position to do this even though he may
have been following instructions from the directors of
The Mother Church. I am sure this man was sincerely
motivated, but I told him that I loved him too much
to place him or anyone else in an embarrassing situation. I was in possession of the harmony of my being
and I was preserving his divine dignity as well. I not
only understood my divinity to be at work, but I understood his was also.

Subsequently by telephone from my branch church
and a letter from The Mother Church in Boston, I was
informed I had been dropped from both memberships
because of having written *The Bridge.* I relate this story
to show how I thought about myself in the circumstance that came to me and how I felt about the visitor
on my doorstep. I could almost see this man one day
daring to read *The Bridge,* even though members have
been warned not to do so. Perhaps he, too, would find
in it something praiseworthy, honest and sincere, and
see it as a book filled with love and inspired by the divine Mind. Within this experience existed an opportunity to realize that in the higher order of love there
was neither the accused nor the accuser. We did not
have to meet under these circumstances; love prepared
another way, and even though its result was excom-
munication for me, I continued to know only the law
of love and harmony to be at work for all.

In my class notes on Identity I said: "Truly, in the higher order of Identity we are the Mind, the I AM, the actual, the potential, the infinite. This Mind is our strength, our perception, our substance, our being. It is our infinite activity, our supply, our intelligence and our love. It enters into every detail of our lives and we, too, possess an awareness of an abiding consciousness of infinite capability."[7]

Just remember when we started out as students in the Science of Being how strong was our desire to be in complete harmony with the understanding of God, Man and the Universe that was given to us in the instruction! Our faithful study for many years, listening to the services, attending lectures and Association addresses, all were part of a glorious possession. For those in need of it, the study and the attendance are still important, but now that we are interested in a higher order *within* Christian Science we have taken steps to advance beyond its rituals and dogma, leaving behind the organization with its instruction based on a premise of dualism. It is on the higher level that *our own understanding* inspires us; it is where we make *our own discoveries;* it is where our true selves are revealed. In this state of spiritual receptivity we see very clearly that the kingdom, the reign of harmony is within us. Our heritage, our birthright, the harmony of our being exists as our very Self.

When Mrs. Eddy says that the reign of harmony *in divine Science* is the kingdom of heaven, don't place this divine Science somewhere outside yourself. From

---

7. Irene S. Moore, C.S.: *Identity,* Copyright 1974. DeVorss & Company, Marina del Rey, California, 90291, page 30.

the study of *The Bridge* and *Identity* you know you
are *all* of it. Scientific knowing provides a place in
your everyday life to entertain its beautiful existence
spiritually and physically. This place is ". . . the realm
of unerring, eternal, and omnipotent Mind; the atmosphere of Spirit, where Soul is supreme"[8] and it is
within you! You exist *as* the atmosphere of Spirit, because you are Spirit where Soul is supreme and, of
course, I am talking here about *your soul.* How close,
how near and dear is this harmony; it cannot be more
intimate to us than it is at this moment. It ". . . is
within reach of man's consciousness here, and the spiritual idea [the Christ of your harmonious being] reveals
it."[9] (Marginal heading: *"The shrine celestial."*)

———————

One day last summer I called someone on the
telephone to invite her to come with her husband to
enjoy our home and the swimming pool. She hesi-
tated at first, going into a lot of detail about how
humid it was where she lived and how she im-
agined it was where I lived, and she asked me what the
temperature was at my home. She expressed surprise
when I lovingly said I was aware only of the atmosphere of God, Good, and the warmth of love. What
would have been gained by a conversation of how it
was at our different homes or about the humidity where
she was which she said was bothering her? I reminded
her again that there could only be a pleasant tempera-

———————

8. *S. & H.* 590:2-3
9. *S. & H.* 576:21-23

ture. Anyway, she and her husband soon came over and it turned out to be a very joyous occasion.

The reason I am sharing this with you is to bring out the need for us to keep the higher thoughts in the forefront of our consciousness. Choosing them properly makes a great difference in the feelings we wish to convey, especially when we are conscious of the soul-sense of our divinity. We have an ability when we speak to select words which are inspiring, helpful, positive and healing. These are in tune with our spirituality and they extend harmoniously into our universe. Voicing them as divine expressions from within brings forth the fruits of our aspirations. Identifying with their true intent, we may watch with marvelous expectancy the freshness of our own divinity expressing itself in the words we select.

"The real Christian Scientist is *constantly* accentuating harmony in word and deed, mentally and orally, perpetually repeating this diapason of heaven: 'Good is my God, and my God is good. Love is my God, and my God is Love.' "[10] And, again, "Speak truly, and each word of thine shall be a fruitful seed . . ."[11]

It is similarly true about the written word. Writing loving thoughts makes them meaningful in our own lives as well as in the lives of those to whom we write. We are actually making these words a glorious personal statement of our true being. "In the beginning was the Word, and the Word was with God, and the Word was God."[12] Identify as this Word; begin today, and see how the ever-present harmony of your being

10. *Mis.* 206:19-23 (Italics mine)
11. *Mis.* 338:28-29
12. *John* 1:1

gives visible meaning to your life in every situation as you express this higher order of your divinity. "A great contribution to my sense of personal identity is my discovery that *I* am the creator of my every word," says John M. Dorsey.[13]

In the chapter in *Science and Health* titled *The Apocalypse,* John, the Revelator, speaks of the spiritual outpouring of bliss and glory he describes as the city which "lieth foursquare." In studying this it becomes clear that this city is not a specific locality where one lives but, rather, a *spiritual habitation* which exists as one's own wholeness, an entirety of Being wherever one may be. "This spiritual, holy habitation . . ."[14] is where we are mentally, physically and spiritually; it is where we live as conscious awareness; it is our own distinct material/spiritual environment. We are not isolated from our surroundings; we are integrated with them and we know them to be real and substantial, materially beautiful in their spirituality.

The *Word,* the *Christ, Christianity,* and *Divine Science* are descriptions of the four sides of our spiritual dwelling. Since it is ". . . the spiritual outpouring of bliss and glory . . ."[15] this is what *we* are and therefore it is *our* spiritual/material habitation, our bliss and our glory. We do not need to be transported into a nether world to live in this dwelling; it is for us here

---

13. John M. Dorsey, M.D.: *Illness or Allness.* Wayne State University Press, Detroit, 1965, p. 56.
14. *S. & H.* 577:12
15. *S. & H.* 574:14-15

in the flesh, humanly alive just as John was. Today, we know *we are* the *Word* in the same way that we see ourselves as the expression of Life, Truth, and Love, and we are the *Christ* for ". . . the spiritual idea reveals it."[16] We are the principle of *Christianity* embodied, the third side of this spiritual habitation, divinity unfolding Christian love in its higher order, providing a way that we as functioning, loving, spiritual ideas are inspired to give and to receive.

The fourth side is *Divine Science,* the higher order which interprets ". . . the Principle of heavenly harmony."[17] Let your divinity recognize the light and glory of your new revelation as a personal illumination, never final, of course, but ever expanding, for there can be no finality in an infinite universe teeming with infinite ideas.

I would like to take a few moments here to tell you about a woman who is present in this class. A friend had given her *Identity* to read and she identified beautifully with its message. When she learned I was having a class on the *Harmony of Being* she asked me if she could attend. Her thought was so clear that I felt she was already demonstrating heights of harmony and love in her everyday life. When I asked her why she thought she should attend the class she said that while she had a God-consciousness awareness of her life at least three quarters of the time she hoped that by at-

---

16. *S. & H.* 576:22-23
17. *S. & H.* 560:11

tending this class on the *Harmony of Being* she would
acquire the last quarter! It was clear that she wanted
her spiritual habitation to be complete, and so sincere
was her desire I did not discuss her reasoning with her,
but I must now emphasize to all who are present today
that there are no quarters to God-consciousness. Oneness is not something to be divided up into parts. Our
recognition of it is consciousness continually revealing
itself in terms of growth, change and movement ahead.
The nature of infinity is such that there is no time when
newness ceases to be. We have often heard there is
nothing new under the sun; true or not, until a thing
is new to *you,* it remains hidden. Perpetual revelation
gives us discoveries that are moving experiences.

––––––––––

Returning to our city foursquare, may I add to its
dimensions an all-embracing atmosphere of divine Love.
In the higher order of *Self* you accept this harmonious
habitation as your very own and you rejoice as it. I
bring the revelator's foursquare city to your attention
because I remember as well as you do all of the metaphysical work we did with its message as students within the instruction of Christian Science. Realizing today
we are this spiritual habitation removes the need for us
to stand in awe of John of Patmos. This occupancy is
our own. You may ask how it can be ours. Well, in
crossing your bridge (coming out of the dualism into
a glorious oneness) you identify spiritually with a new
premise. You understand it and you come naturally into
the harmony of your being, experiencing the glory and
the bliss which is rightfully yours.

In the description of the city as having four sides, these are not the walls we may imagine them to be for it is also said they have no boundary or limit. Thus they have a spiritual dimension which is infinite. Love is the city's light (that light must be you) and divine Mind (your mind) its forever interpreter. The higher order of Body indicates this holy, harmonious habitation to be the temple (body) which *you* are. On page 576 of *Science and Health*, Mrs. Eddy speaks of this temple (body) as *the shrine celestial*. Accept this grand idea of yourself now in the flesh. John Dorsey also speaks inspiringly about this:

> The divinity of every person is always present, but to be most effective it must be seen by him.
>
> Everyone who learns to appreciate his life must undergo an it's-to-good-to-be-true stage of self-appraisal.[18]

It is more than just an interesting observation that *Revelation* is the last book of the New Testament. In this study of the Bible we have read the *Word*, we have understood the fulfilling concepts of the *Christ*, we have embraced *Christianity* and have advanced naturally to *Divine Science*. Therefore the full import of Truth is now yours to live. This New Jerusalem, the reign of harmony, shows you the spiritual fact of your present liveable reality. In it we find the higher order of our Spiritual Habitation. We do not deal with the

---

18. John M. Dorsey, M.D.: *Illness or Allness*. Copyright 1965, Wayne State University Press, Detroit, Michigan 48202, page 184.

previous instruction in dualism; we have progressed
out of this. Now we become aware of our personal-
spiritual, harmonious Oneness, and we learn how to relate to the universe in which we live.

I appreciated a letter from a person who said this
very well: "I have long considered the dualism of Mrs.
Eddy most unfortunate. It is so wonderful of you to hit
the upper, positive octave. Strange enough, I am sure
that Mary Baker Eddy would very much approve." To
this I agree. Mrs. Eddy pointed out the higher consciousness in her Science, the very same which I am
promoting in a practical and progressive way. This
higher view is present in many of her works awaiting
an underlining for greater emphasis in your life. Another person wrote: "Let me say how grateful I am
for your two books. They have uncovered so much for
me. Bringing up to the surface the idea of duality has
been such a clarifying thought. For years I've been
puzzled by such statements as 'Spirit is the *real* and
eternal' — then 'matter is the unreal and temporal.'
Why? I've drawn many lines through the negative
statements, feeling sort of sneaky at doing so, but now
I'm sure."

Of course all letters that come to me are not necessarily so positive about seeing "through the negative
statements." A friend of mine wrote to me of the time
she brought up my name with one of her acquaintances and how ominously dead was the silence that
followed. Having told this person a little about my
books, my friend asked whether she had read them.
"No, I have not," she said, "because they are against
Christian Science." My friend asked her how she could

say this if she had not read them, and then asked her who had told her such a thing. The answer was "The Mother Church." She pressed on: "How can you deprive yourself of your divine right of thinking and choosing for yourself? If you have the same opinion after you have read Irene's books I will respect it, but to say that the church is telling you what you can and cannot read is taking away your right to choose." Her friend thought about this for awhile. Although agreeing with her argument, she said she must abide by the church rules. My correspondent went on, informing her that for one thing Jesus never laid down any rules about what one should read. Furthermore, if she ever did read the books and found one word that was not full of love she was professing she wanted, my friend said she would like to know about it. I finally wrote to this correspondent thanking her for her loving efforts of persuasion. Yet I am completely assured that when a student is ready the message appears. I rejoice in knowing that the message of the Higher Order of Science remains always ready for free spirits wherever and whoever they are. With honest hearts they assuredly will seek their highest level of consciousness, reaching for the harmony they deserve.

Interesting articles have come to me for many years. In fact they still come to me, and I like to share them. Perhaps the passage from a manuscript which I am going to read to you now has already been presented to you. In any event let me give it to you again. The manuscript was found in Egypt on the reverse side of a landsurveyor's list of measurements. It is kept in the British Museum, secured in a case which is chained to a table. An officer stands by it at all times. He allows

anyone to copy it but not to touch it. This is part of
the message:

> Jesus said: "Let not him who seeketh cease
> from seeking until he hath found:
> . . . and when he hath found, he shall be
> amazed.
> . . . and when he hath been amazed, he shall
> reign,
> . . . and when he shall reign, he shall rest.
> . . . The kingdom of heaven is within you
> and whosoever shall know himself, shall find
> it.
> . . . Strive therefore to know yourselves and
> ye shall know ye are the City of God, and
> ye are the City."

The "City of God" is the same that St. John The
Divine tells us about in the chapter in *Revelation*—
the city foursquare. This heavenly city—which we understand to be the New Jerusalem—is interesting to
comment upon if we look at page 576 of *Science and
Health,* lines 4 to 7: ". . . this New Jerusalem, this infinite All, which to us seems hidden in the midst of
remoteness,—reached St. John's vision while yet he
tabernacled with mortals." In the higher order of Science this is not hidden from us any longer. Do not get
so mystical about it that you consider it something beyond your sense experience, something too ambiguous
to be attainable in your present life. It is a very real,
factual, marvelous development of ourselves as *our*
Word, *our* Christ, *our* Christianity, and *our* Divine

Science all held together as Love. The higher order of
Revelation provides a reason for this knowledge about
ourselves as this spiritual habitation. As you read "And
I . . . saw these things, and heard them. And when I
had heard and seen, I fell down to worship before the
feet of the angel which shewed me these things,"[19] remember that this angel is your own consciousness, the
awareness of your own divinity. Appreciate it for all
its glory. Never mind about John of Patmos now. The
important thing is that *you* are seeing and hearing
these things, and *your* God-consciousness (angel
thought) is revealing great truths to you just as angel
thoughts revealed them to John. We recognize this divine cognition going on within us; we know all things
are ours to see just as John saw them. Mrs. Eddy valued
his revelation greatly. She says: ". . . his vision is the
acme of . . . [Christian] Science as the Bible reveals
it."[20]

We cannot hear it enough: "The kingdom of heaven
is within you,"—this harmony of life and therefore this
wholeness, this naturalness, this simplicity, this peaceful habitation, this joy, fulfillment and satisfaction.
These are ours because "In divine Science, *man* pos-
sesses this recognition of harmony consciously in pro-
portion to his understanding of God,"[21] and we are
that man. Identifying one's human self as the holy
habitation is *knowing God in a new way;* it is asserting the fact that your very own God-Self is your present, personal/spiritual existence, and this assertion
establishes an eternal foundation for the harmony of

---

19. *Revelation* 22:8
20. *S. & H.* 577:30-31
21. *S. & H.* 576:23-25 (Italics mine).

your life. *The Bridge*[22] brings this understanding to
you in a very descriptive and practical way. In other
words, do not let the wonderful revelation in the Bible
be limited to John's experience. It is describing your
own, your present, everyday, physical, life experience
of heaven on earth. Accept it as yours; go beyond John,
allowing the vision to expand with your increased understanding of the higher order of Science. This is
yourself as the vision. One day my friend, Allen Boone,
author of *Kinship With All Life,* said that it isn't
essential any more to know what the Gospel means
to Matthew, Mark, Luke or John, but what it means
to us in this life of ours.

Let us recapitulate: In agreement with our higher
order of Self-Revelation we are the full and complete
expression of ". . . I AM; the all-knowing, all-seeing,
all-acting, all-wise, all-loving, and eternal; Principle;
Mind; Soul; Spirit; Life; Truth; Love; all substance;
intelligence."[23] We are the divine sense of Deity and
we enjoy this identity, this holy habitation, this harmony as our individual divinity and we possess it forever.

It was wonderful to read this in a letter from some
one who had just finished reading *Identity* and who is
presently in this class:

> Your brave book *Identity* has enabled me for
> the first time to glimpse the fact that I am all
> the synonyms for God—something that I had

---

22. Irene S. Moore, C.S.: *The Bridge.* Published 1971, DeVorss & Co.,
Marina del Rey, California 90291.
23. *S. & H.* 587:5-8

not realized before! Then it follows: If I am all these things (qualities), how could I ever condemn myself? . . . I was subconsciously always trying to exchange an inharmonious condition for a harmonious one. You have said, "Why replace something with Truth when something is *already* Truth?" Wonderful! No more grasping for what we desire to be — only realizing what we *are.* Yes, our "work" is very different now from what it was in the orthodox teaching.

> With Happiness (happiness)
> and Love (love).

I was delighted the way the letter was signed for it showed me he had understood the full import of the use of capitalization that I bring out in *Identity,* pp 10, 108.

———

Let us illustrate the personalization of the power of the Word which entered a woman's consciousness when she came to see me one day. She told me that she had been a very faithful Christian Scientist, attending church services for years and working on many committees, but she felt that Life, Truth and Love as she understood them from her instruction were not continuing to be as acceptable as they had once been. She discussed her situation, informing me how saddened she was by the many problems confronting her and of her inability to cope with them, one of which was an illness that had not been met in Christian Science. She felt guilty and frustrated. I asked her if she thought all of this was her highest expression of God—her highest understanding of Life as she knew it. She quickly said, "Oh, no!" She was surprised when I informed her that *her present experience was her highest understanding* of Good because there is no other expression, but I reminded her that there could surely be a higher one than what she was seeing at that moment. In any event all appearances had to be the appearances of God, since God is ALL. To think otherwise would be to admit the presence of another power than good. Sometimes it is not easy to see this, but as one does the appearances soon coincide with the seeing.

She thought of the words "restoring" and "renewing," and then the word "resuscitation" came to her. She found its meaning helpful and accepted it as it related personally to her in a spiritual way: ". . . in Science one must understand the resuscitating law of Life. This is the *seed within itself* bearing fruit after its kind, spoken of in Genesis."[24] Listening to these words she understood that the Science *within herself* was the spiritual exploration and acceptance she needed for her situation, and she began to see that there was nothing to stand in the way of ". . . spiritual power to resuscitate [herself] . . ."[25] She did not have to get her personal self out of the way for her spiritual self to appear; both were present at the same time, and with this knowledge she could be ready to accept the harmony of her being.

Knowing herself to be the structure of Truth meant

24. *S. & H.* 180:8-10 (Italics mine).
25. *S. & H.* 365:29-30

that she did not have to go anywhere to get it. Nor did
she need to do anything this moment other than to accept wholeheartedly the fact of this spiritual law of
life and love: the God within her operating and functioning marvelously as her Self. She consented to these
truths and then added, "Why, I have been worrying
myself to death! But now I know I don't need to do
that anymore." She smiled for the first time during her
visit. I asked her to tell me all she knew about life as it
pertained to her divinity, and as she spoke her sadness
left her. The magnitude of her illness diminished, the
harmony of her being presented itself to her and with
it I saw her confidence return. Her God-Self was in
possession. Before leaving she was assured with certainty that everything which had enriched her life was
still enriching it, and when she left she had an increased
value of her health and her holiness as the rightful
state of her Being.

The harmony of one's divinity is always as close to
him as his own breath. Angel thoughts come to our
consciousness bringing themselves to recognition because they are already known to us. The definition for
"angels" is in the *Glossary* and the part that I am most
receptive to is this: ". . . spiritual intuitions, pure and
perfect; the inspiration of goodness, purity, and immortality . . ."[26] The higher order of Ourselves pre-
pares us to receive these marvelous intuitions coming
to us daily and the same order directs how we should
act upon them. Acknowledge these inspirations by doing something about them. Joyously open the door of

---

26. *S. & H.* 581:4-6

consciousness to feel their presence and power! Welcome them and experience wonderful happenings!

I want everyone here to know that should a momentary sense of discouragement or fear, failure or disappointment appear to you, there is an immediate recourse for you, namely: your insistance that you are not overcome by it—not at all. You are warmly possessed by the rescuscitating law of life within; the reign of harmony, the law of love is asserting itself wherever you are. You are at peace. You must remember *you are your own practitioner!* Treat every situation as an opportunity to call upon your very own angel (harmonious) thoughts of God-love. They sustain you always because they are pure and perfect. Purity and perfection admit no sadness. Remember "God's in his heaven; all's right with the world," and it is your world that is alright! With heaven (harmony) as your habitation you have reason to rejoice! REJOICE!

In the final paragraphs from *My Young Years,* Arthur Rubinstein writes: "I am very lucky, but I have a little theory about this. I have noticed through experience and through my own observations that Providence, Nature, God, or what I would call the Power of Creation seems to favor human beings who accept and love life *unconditionally.* And I am certainly one who does, with all my heart. So I have discovered as a result of what I can only call miracles that whenever my inner self desires something subconsciously, life will somehow grant it to me."[27] I have italicized the word "unconditionally" to emphasize my feeling that he means

27. Arthur Rubinstein: *My Young Years,* Alfred A. Knopf, Inc., New York, copyright 1973.

absolutely, confidently, completely and *ideally*. Arthur Rubinstein is talking about people who accept life without reservation. In this forthright way his "Power of Creation" favors us with what he calls miracles. In the higher order of Science we see these events as harmonious concomitants to correct scientific knowing.

In this light I would like to speak for a moment about our government and how we may be inclined to think and feel and know about it. Much is being said these days that would disturb our peace, to divide us, or to make us feel discouraged regarding the functioning of our great Republic. Well, at such times the same law of restoration we are talking about in relation to personal life works in government as well. We do not outline how the law operates. Its method of fulfillment follows in direct relation to the breadth of our opportunities to bless it. Goodness does not need our guidance to pursue its best course, but we have to be expectant of God, Good.

All action of law is salutary. We keep our thoughts filled with the law of love for all branches of our government, and because we elect members of congress we are responsible for supporting its best ideas and its highest ideals. Love, the bountiful law of life, renews, restores, and resuscitates. It heals at all times, and because the government is on God's shoulders it is on our shoulders as well. Our trust in the law to operate at its highest level emphasizes the truth of the motto we find on all our currencies: "In God we trust."

Of course our work in the higher order of government is to keep our thoughts in tune as Truth and Love where they belong. Mrs. Eddy says "Truth [which we

are] is affirmative, and confers harmony."[28] She also
states that "The universe of Spirit is peopled with
spiritual beings, and its government is divine Science,"[29]
and since "Man is the offspring, not of the lowest, but
of the highest qualities of Mind,"[30] we keep this man
(ourselves) and our mankind on the level that includes
pure motives and honest endeavor as our spiritual nature. Our spiritual sense embraces all that we are, so
as citizens we have a very special work to do bearing
witness to Truth as it applies to our republic. With an
inner harmony to bless all we are able to express our
thoughts constructively so that events and conclusions
conform to our highest consciousness of good. Let our
words be expressed lovingly at all times. The harmony
of our Being is the Saviour to ourselves and in turn,
therefore, to our government.

Several years ago I went to visit a woman I had
known for quite a long time. When I walked in her
door, I noticed she was just turning off her television
set. She said she had been listening to Senator John
Kennedy who was then a candidate for the presidency
of our country. She told me she was disturbed by the
fact that he was a Roman Catholic and that he might
be our next President.

I had the opportunity at that moment to accept the
harmony of her being as a spiritual fact and to know
that divine love as her spiritual, peaceful nature was
even then doing its perfect work. What she called a
disturbance in herself was actually the presence of Love
making itself known. I reminded her of our premise

---

28. *S. & H.* 418:20-21
29. *S. & H.* 264:32 to 265-1
30. *S. & H.* 265:1-3

that "All is infinite Mind and its infinite manifestation . . ."[31] and I told her that as we hold to this spiritual fact *we see in Science the perfect man manifest!* This meant that her view of perfection had to include Senator Kennedy as a person; otherwise where would the man of God's creation be? Her receptivity was immediate. She said she always had thought of "perfect *man*," to which Mrs. Eddy has often referred, as an ideal far removed from persons as we know them. Her concept of *man* had been so spiritual that she could not possibly associate it with someone walking around in the flesh! Yet she had to admit it is always a person in the flesh which is healed. "Jesus beheld in Science the perfect man . . ." (*S. & H.* 476:32 to 477:1) and it *was this perfect man as person* that he healed. Who else could this man be than a mortal being? The healings accorded to Jesus occurred before the very eyes of others. They saw them happen with their mortal vision which revealed to them the same perfection of man that was revealed to Jesus.

There is a sequel to this story which I feel is most important. On the day President Kennedy was assassinated she telephoned me, recalling the conversation we had had about divine love's presence as her own divinity and Senator Kennedy's divinity also. She said she realized how important it had been for her to have a change of attitude and she added that she would have been most saddened on this particular day if she had held to her earlier opinions and judgmental attitudes. It was clear that through this experience she had learned much of the higher order of love as it applies

31. *S. & H.* 468:10-11

to persons in her everyday experience. She had grown
to realize the necessity of holding to the harmony of
her being for herself as well as for her mankind.

In a remarkable book, *Kinship With All Life,* by
Allen Boone, we are told how to "clean the slate" for
everyone *even including a fly,* which he names Freddie.
We read:

> One morning as Freddie was watching me
> shave, an idea came to me. It was this: that
> for me to know that my little companion ex-
> isted at all, he first had to appear as an image
> in my individual mind. Otherwise I could not
> possibly be aware of him. First I must identify
> him as a mental image or idea, and then pro-
> ject that mental picture from the subjective
> into the objective state . . . .
> The first thing I did after recognizing the far-
> reaching significance of all this was to wash
> Freddie's record slate completely clean. I
> erased all unfavorable qualifications, all judg-
> ments having to do with him as a fly. Off
> went everything that I had ever heard, read
> or thought about flies that was in the least bit
> restricting or unkind. It was a thorough purg-
> ing. From then on it was I, not "public opin-
> ion," who did the writing on Freddie's life
> slate. From then on he became to me what I,
> and I alone, thought about him. And that sus-
> tained attitude toward my little companion
> opened the way for all the remarkable things
> which subsequently happened.
> Another factor that was helpful in getting us

past the blockages that have prevented humans and flies from really understanding each other was this motto: "If you would learn the secret of right relations, look only for the good, that is, the divine, in people and things . . ."[32]

Aren't these wonderful thoughts to project into our world of ideas? May I remind you of the way we worked with the person having a problem with *Benjamin* in our class on *Identity*.[33] Remember how we accepted the second part of the definition for *Benjamin* as our starting premise? In looking again at Allen Boone's book we see that it doesn't matter whether we are dealing with a politician, a lawyer, a doctor, an animal or even an *insect*—we start out with the perfection of Being. We ". . . look only for . . . the divine, in people and things . . ." and from it comes the kinship with all life that expresses a universal harmony. So we must think this way about our Republic and our universe of nature as well as about the people we know.

How many higher order references to government there are in Mrs. Eddy's writings! No wonder I want to preserve the higher order which I find in them. Let me share this one with you and then let us accept the full meaning in its relation to ourselves. "The revered President and Congress of our favored land are in God's hands."[34] They must therefore be in our hands as well. A wonderful meaning for the word "hand" is

32. J. Allen Boone: *Kinship With All Life.* Harper & Row, Publishers, New York, 16, New York, Copyright 1954, pp 142, 143.
33. Irene S. Moore, C.S.: *Identity*, pp 86, 87, 88.
34. *My.* 278:13-14

power, spiritual might. Exercise your spiritual power by holding to our Republic's highest ideals, not emotionally or with prejudice but with a *realistic optimism* voicing the divine love which you are. Spiritual perfection, intuition, knowledge, choice, direction embrace all that we are, so as citizens we have a very special work to do.

As we hold in consciousness our highest concept of government we think constructively, emphasizing our views within the framework of our identity as Truth and Love. Of course we always have the right to question motives and actions just as we can question them at church meetings or anywhere else. This is what democracy stands for. It is always our spiritual sense which questions and inquires, and this spiritual sense gives us the courage to say what we believe and to say it in a loving way. When one knows *he is* Truth, he can speak confidently as well as lovingly. To illustrate, let me relate how one person expressed this love courageously at a church meeting.

When I was treasurer of the Greenwich (Connecticut) Church, we found on a certain occasion that our financial situation was so unstable that we actually had an operational deficit. Something had to be done about it so a special meeting was called. After the reading from the desk, the financial report was given and the meeting was opened to remarks by the members. The very first man who spoke said that before this meeting he had inquired of The Executive Board about the financial situation and in the course of conversation he had asked what salaries were being paid in addition to other expenses. He reported his surprise on learning that so little was being paid its several officers and right then and there he made a motion to *increase* all the salaries! This was his response to the financial situation! The motion was put to a vote and was immediately carried. Not one word was mentioned by any members about the deficit. The courage of this one individual had raised the consciousness of the members to one of gratitude, eclipsing any thought of deficiency. From that time on we never had a financial problem. As a matter of fact the membership soon after took on a commitment to purchase a new organ which cost $18,000, and it was installed while I was the treasurer. Spiritual sense does not interest itself in deficits because it has *so much surplus!*

I do not mean that we make believe situations do not exist which are unpleasant or depleting. This is not our work in the Higher Order of Science. When they do appear, however, we accept them as opportunities for us to bring into action the harmony that is present all the while. Our scientific minds love to be used for positive approaches to experiences testing our God-potential. We may well remember this at such times: Trials simply demonstrate our understanding of love. We do not ignore them or "say it isn't so." We know the substantiality of Truth about them and we consider these occasions as demands that the rewarding lessons be shown to us.

In the story I have just related about the deficit in the church, we were simply told to show more gratitude (love) for what was being done by those members in positions of responsibility. It was an illustration of divine love leading us to more expansive attitudes. The member who spoke so scientifically brought the entire membership to the infinite supply level of consciousness.

I would like to point out that in our work as the higher order of scientific reasoning we do not acknowledge the first part of Mrs. Eddy's Scientific Statement of Being, namely that "There is no life, truth, intelligence nor substance in matter..." because we *know* today that matter and its material manifestation *is spiritual substance*. Substance makes its practical appearance in ways our spiritual senses now accept! The acceptance of this as fact brings us the harmony of our being. On the other hand, if you are still holding to what I have just quoted as Truth, you are still in the elementary instruction of Christian Science and its premise of dualism. Your consecrated work suffices to lift you out of the negations through translation into the positive divine essence of substance.

In Points to Ponder, a section to be found in the *Reader's Digest* for August, 1974, I read an interesting quote by Howard Whitman:

> A wise physician said to me, "I have been practicing medicine for 30 years, and I have prescribed many things. But for most of what ails the human creature the best medicine is love."
> "What if it doesn't work"? I asked.
> "Double the dose," he replied.[35]

---

35. Excerpts from *Points to Ponder* by Howard Whitman. The Register and Tribune Syndicate, Inc., Des Moines, Iowa. The *Reader's Digest*, August 1974. "Howard Whitman reprinted by permission."

The apostle Paul, in his message to the Philippians, says:

> ... whatsoever things are true, whatsoever things are honest, whatsoever things are just, whatsoever things are pure, whatsoever things are lovely, whatsoever things are of good report; ... *think on these things* ...[36]

It is my desire to keep my consciousness filled as Truth and Love, and my work is to put these qualities of Mind into practice moment by moment. In the higher order of Science we have the capacity to be the presence of Truth and Love, so we keep our minds filled with worthwhile attributes: things that are true, things that are *honest* and *just* and *pure* and of *good report*. Hold to them! Fill your minds with them; find yourselves experiencing the inner happiness that follows! It is good to have concrete experiences which point out these moments for by giving them recognition they remain with us to strengthen our trust. We appreciate these harmonious angel-thoughts which come from our own withinness.

My husband and I were traveling in Europe on the 9th day of August, 1974, when news reports announced Richard Nixon's resignation. Our friends on the cruise expressed different opinions about it. On that particular day we were scheduled to visit the Carl Milles Gardens in Stockholm, but having been there several years before, we decided to go on another tour. As the motor coach drove off I knew that I was not going

---

36. *Philippians* 4:8. (Italics mine).

to add to the burden of our nation by having judgmental attitudes, nor by contending with good-versus-
evil concepts, nor would I entertain criticism or dismay. I had an opportunity to be a blessing to this report, keeping my own thoughts in tune with love by
holding consistently to my understanding of *Man, Present Being,* the title and substance of one of the chap-
ters in *The Bridge.*

I recalled one of the sculptured pieces that was going to be seen by many that day at the Carl Milles
Gardens in Stockholm. It had impressed me very much
when I first saw it; there was something very spiritual
about it and in my memory on the day of Mr. Nixon's
resignation it meant even more. The bronze sculpture
is a life-size figure of a man held high against the sky
by an enormous hand, confidently balancing the man
between its thumb and index finger. The man's gaze
is directed upwards to the sky. The sculpture is called
The Hand of God. It seemed to me that my work was
to place Richard Nixon in a similar state of grace.
Holding my President there was the best I could do
for him in the higher order of love and by keeping this
thought I would be helping to bring a harmony in the
changes that would follow. This was not to indicate
an approval or disapproval of him. It was my way of
giving the situation that was presenting itself its greatest opportunity for good. I am relating this today to
show the quality of thought I held to bring in the
higher order of my Science.

Now I would like to read a poem by Elena Goforth
Whitehead under the heading of *Fraternity.* It expresses the feelings I had as I recalled thoughts of this
statue by Carl Milles in relation to Richard Nixon's

decision to resign. The poem is as completely descriptive of my sentiments of this event as any poem could be.

I ADD TO THE WHOLE

All people grow as one fraternal race.
The common mind ascends eternally.
My thoughts and acts must never slow the pace
Of those who share the upward road with me.
Who knows the burdens other persons bear?
I will not add my weight of reprimand.
No joy shall feel the chill of my despair.
No hope shall be disheartened by my hand.
All people are my priceless counterparts.
All roads converge, and all lives intertwine.
I know the place where world improvement starts:
The private self. I lift the state of mine.
Contributing the height I manifest,
I raise the mind in which the nations rest.[37]

Well, what has all this to do with the Harmony of Being? Again I remind you: an advanced student is unable to work with the old tools. He cannot be casting out error, or devil, by removing the personal sense of man (which we used to term corporeality) and then putting in its place the man of God's annointing: the incorporeal, divine and immortal who is *invisible to our mortal sight!* This dualistic approach never did give us a solution for the man we saw as person did

---

37. Elena Goforth Whitehead: *Attitudes.* Privately Printed, Copyright, 1973, 378 Belmont Street, Oakland, California 94610, page 25.

not leave our sight no matter how persistently we tried
to have him lose his mortality. The point of healing
rests only on our *beholding* in Science *the perfect man,*
and unless we see this man as *all men at this moment
perfect,* it is impossible to come into the kingdom
(harmony of being). If we cast out devils in one direction we find them popping up in another, and with
this going on how can we hold unreservedly to "The
divine understanding reigns, is *all,* and there is no other
consciousness"?[38]

A man cannot have two masters. He must hold
tenaciously to the consciousness of the higher order of
Science, maintaining not only a broader sense of personal love but also establishing universal Truth within
himself as his present Reality. Our Science is not abstract. It is a practical, demonstrable, living science,
and we are spiritual fact finders! These many stories
I am relating help to show how important it is to keep
our minds occupied with truth and love consistently.
Accepting the divine mind as our present consciousness
is precisely what brings about the Harmony of our
Being.

Many of the Pharisees were perplexed when Jesus
told them that the kingdom of God was at hand, and
even more when he said it was *within* them. If we read
Matthew 23:13 we see that Jesus knew some of them had
". . . shut up the kingdom of heaven against men . . ."
for he told them ". . . ye neither go in *yourselves,*
neither suffer ye them that are entering to go in." For
the most part they did not understand the Oneness concept. The dualism present in their own teaching pre-

---

38. *S. & H.* 536:8-9

vented them from "entering," so they naturally were
out to silence the new teacher who was showing others
how *to live* the kingdom of God, the harmony of their
being, *here on earth*. This "living" required a state of
consciousness in each individual which would acknowledge divinity in humanness, and this was a very un-
conventional idea at that time.

Of course this was difficult for the Pharisees to comprehend because their concepts had indoctrinated them
with contrary beliefs. To them the kingdom of God
was very far removed from any person walking around
in the flesh. The Old Testament prophets taught that
the Messiah was yet to come and would "restore all
things" including a heaven-on-earth. You and I know
today that the Messiah is the Christ *within* us, renewing our consciousness through our identification as
spiritual truth and by way of personal experience.

Now the idea of restoration is referred to by Mrs.
Eddy in the definition of *Elias* in the *Glossary* of *Science and Health*. She interprets this prophet as follows:
"Prophecy; spiritual evidence opposed to material
sense; Christian Science, with which can be discerned
the spiritual fact of whatever the material senses behold; the basis of immortality. 'Elias truly shall first
come, and restore all things.' (Matthew 17:11)." How
many times have you read this, obediently accepting
the first part but unable to get beyond its duality to
justify the higher thought in the second part? Today
we need not wait for Elias to ". . . come, and restore
all things." We bring ourselves to the glorious perception of the *spiritual fact* of ". . . whatever the material senses behold . . ." The higher order of Personal
Prophecy insists that we make this identification. The

glorious restoration of person, place and thing is precisely our new approach to life! We are presently seeing the spiritual fact of these appearing in our material universe through the proper understanding of our physical/spiritual world of reality.

In the definition of *Elias* given above we are presented with two separate and differing ideas. If you choose the first one where ". . . spiritual evidence [is] opposed to material sense . . ." you really are not in a position to include the second part of the quotation. You blocked it out by accepting the first part. This illustrates the dualism I have found often in the instruction of Christian Science. Your harmony of being eludes you if you are still *feuding* with material sense. This type of metaphysics belongs to orthodox Christian Science. On the other hand in our work we use materiality for its intrinsic worth instead of considering it erroneous and unreal, and the intrinsic worth of material sense is its spiritual fact! Spiritual/material sense is One. If you get rid of material sense you *remove a part of the whole*. It is the quarrel with matter that must be eliminated, for materiality is not at all in contention with spirit. The idea of its contentiousness belongs in the elementary instruction of Christian Science; it is not for the graduate. Our senses are not opposed to anything; they are in accord with *all we experience*.

So, as you study this definition of Elias it becomes clear that from our premise that "All is infinite Mind and its infinite manifestation . . ." the reference to spiritual-evidence-versus-material-sense must be translated out of its traditional meaning. We have already done our metaphysical work with it in the instruction and have redeemed our senses into the spiritual evidences of their divinity. Spiritual and physical restoration occur as Truth is seen for itself.

Jesus offered his kingdom (harmony) to the people around him. Whether they were in the midst of wars, national distress, or perplexities of all kinds, he told them to *look up* to a higher concept of life. In many instances those hearing him preferred not to do so, but the receptive ones did. Some were predicting where and when the kingdom would come, but he made it clear that it did not come with their type of outlining. His kingdom was to come to those who had a spiritually correct state of mind, an attitude of personal God-consciousness which would apply the higher order of Science in daily work. Having this, he said, would bring harmony to believers, producing the peace, joy and confidence that characterize fulfillment. As we *look up* to our highest conception of being we find this living love, the God-Idea, peace and productivity, residing always where they belong: within us.

———

Let us take a statement from *Job* 22:21: "Acquaint now thyself with *him,* and be at peace: thereby good shall come unto thee." Who is this "him"? In doctrinal Christian Science the "him" referred to is God, the incorporeal, divine and immortal concept of Truth. We were taught to consecrate ourselves after this ideal as best we could in our mortality. Now, of course, we know that with *the traditional understanding* of "him" as taught in Christian Science it is impossible for us to see ourselves in our present mortality as any more than a misconception of truth striving for higher at-

tainments. But the relationship so lovingly offered us
in this statement from Job really comes to us from a
true understanding of *ourselves*. The immortal and
spiritual presence of our divine being as peace and joy
is the "him" *within us* which asks for recognition. Until we accept this we can strive forever to be lifted out
of mortality because at the same time we are admitting
the limitation that materiality gives us. Understanding
the truth about ourselves removes the barrier.

This brings to mind the advertisement I wrote about
in *Identity* on page 15. It was from *The Los Angeles
Times* about a movie called *The Ruling Class*. Someone is asking one of the characters how he knows he is
God. And his answer is: "Simple. When I pray *to Him*
I find I'm talking to myself." And I added "Isn't this
enlightening! An appeal to God is *an appeal to the
higher order of One's Self!*" The thought may be new
to some, and I would advise those who are not at ease
with it to continue with their work in orthodox Christian Science instruction until the facts of truth advance
them to a more personal awareness of their God-consciousness.

We know that in the higher order of intelligent,
harmonious being, the peace and joy we seek is always
found within us, and as we go on with our glorious, personal identification, accepting the harmony of our being, we joyously renounce statements which are no
longer in accord with our elevated spirit. Then new
visions are experienced; new ways of seeing things appear from *one's personal Mount of Revelation,* not
from Jesus', the gospel writers, or from "him", but
from one's spiritual awareness of his divine life. This
does not mean that we fail to appreciate the contribu-

tion these men have made from their own revelation. What was given to them was in turn revealed to us by them. The important thing that is happening now is that we imbibe the spirit, we understand, we identify and walk on into *our vision infinite.* This is what spiritual unfoldment does for us.

> A person arrives at the peak of sanity when he consciously comes only to himself, for only then does he cultivate the true meaning of life, his life. The only *possible* "authority," or sane theocratic conception, is the divine right of the individual being.[39]

A woman writes:

> After studying Science less than a year, I suddenly came to the conclusion that if all the things I had been reading, for example, that man has dominion, then I was a good deal more than merely a "reflection." I tried talking to different practitioners and students about this without a satisfying explanation. Imagine my surprise when reading your book, *The Bridge,* I found on page 136 that (in the higher order of Science) there is no "reflection" as it is understood in Christian Science. What a relief!

Later this same woman wrote again. This time she said:

---

39. John M. Dorsey, M.D.: *Illness or Allness,* Wayne State University Press, Detroit, 1965 p. 564.

I bought a new copy of *Science and Health*
and I am marking it up for myself—for instance, page 76: "When being is understood,
Life will be recognized as infinite—as God,
universal good." I drew red lines under these
lines and crossed out "neither material nor
finite but . . ." I intend to do this all through
the book. What fun to have my own *Science
and Health! Now* when the word reflection
appears in the periodicals or the textbook, I
substitute either the word "manifestation" or
"evidence," as we certainly are the evidence
of God (spirit) made "visible as matter," as
Mr. Booker says in *Notebook #102*.[40]

The conclusion to her letters states:

I'll never forget the time I told a Christian
Science acquaintance that I finally realized
that if God was all, then all there was to me
was God. But she said No to this, that I was
saying that I was God, so I didn't argue . . .

The woman who wrote these letters has stepped
into her higher order of Being and she certainly is enjoying it. She knows the peace and fulfillment which
is ours as we accept the fact that ". . . divine understanding reigns, is *all,* and there is no other consciousness."[41]

40. Richard Booker: *Notebook #102,* 1309 Chicago Avenue, Evanston,
Illinois 60201.
41. *S. & H.* 536:8-9

The German mystic Meister Eckhart says:

Man, yes, I stood with God before time and
the world were created; yes, I was included
in the eternal Godhead even before it became
God. Together with me God has created and
is still and always creating. Only through me
He became God."[42]

In voicing my higher order of Science, I feel that I
am actually preserving and promoting the purity we
find within Christian Science, and I suppose it is the
great inspiration I have found there that makes me
want to share this absolute experience with whoever
is ready for it. Since it is important for students to
challenge any form of restriction found within the
orthodox view, I lovingly show them how great an opportunity they have to accept their God-Being-Self as
"infinity, freedom, harmony, and boundless bliss."[43]
After all, what good would it be to leave one's highest
discovery of this Science unspoken, unwritten, hidden
in one's self unavailable to others of like mind? So I
write, and I speak, and I share very personally what
has come to me as a way to the harmony of Being.
The impersonality of my Science I have put off for a
more personal individuality and freedom to which dogma is often a restraint. When I think this is so, I feel
free to subtract from or add to its form and content

---

42. John M. Dorsey, M.D.: *Illness or Allness.* Wayne State Univ. Press,
Detroit, 1965, p. 60-61.
43. *S. & H.* 481:3-4

according to my spiritual understanding within the new directives of the Oneness concept evolving for me.

We must express ourselves by questioning doctrine whenever we find it is not in accord with our spiritual heights. There is nothing new about this. The Lutheran Church would not exist if Martin Luther had not questioned the authority and the limitations of his own church. His cardinal doctrine was "justification through the merits of Jesus Christ, by Faith alone."[44] This was an emphasis on the personal faith he was proposing for the individual. He was responsible for "completing . . . [a] translation of the whole Bible into the vernacular,"[44] meaning writing the Bible in words that could be read by everyone, thereby giving the individual the right to interpret it according to his own understanding and inspiration. Luther's translation enabled many to make a wider identity for themselves because they did not have to depend on what someone else told them. He gave broader meanings to thoughts of "mercy" and "faith." According to James McDaniel, "Luther threw himself on God's mercy, trusting in His love. He wrote later that it was like being 'reborn' or going through open doors into Paradise."[44] He promoted a personal relationship to his God and in so doing he prepared the way for others.

There would be no Methodism today without movement away from the established Church of England into the more individual religious creed of John Wesley. "Methodism is regarded as a revival of primitive Christian doctrine, fellowship, and discipline. The

44. James McDaniel: *Martin Luther—A Magnet For All Christians,* *Reader's Digest,* Jan. 1968.

Methodist preachers taught a full, free and present salvation as the privilege of every man through faith alone
in Jesus Christ."[45] My own early training in religion
was in this Protestant church and I look back on it in
gladness for the instruction I received as a child. In
Identity I tell of my later meeting with Christian Science and the effect it had on my developing religious
concepts as an adult.

Mary Baker Eddy's initial contribution was to reveal
a *Science* she discovered within her former religious
understanding and it was her desire to share this interpretation. It is interesting to note from the concordances that her early statements on formalized religion are few in comparison to the many references to
her newly discovered *Science*. It was the *Science* of
Christianity she was primarily interested in and, as we
have been informed many times, it was founded on
The Bible. She says ". . . when the spiritual sense of
the creed was discerned in the *Science* of Christianity,
this spiritual sense was . . . the living, palpitating presence of Christ, Truth, which healed the sick."[46]

There are many other instances of people who departed from their religious roots; these are just a few.
But their particular insights dictated the steps they
took and in each case the leaders of these new views
demonstrated a need to be participants instead of just
spectators. They presented the idea of involvement in
religious work through a stronger sense of personal
identity with the ideas that were available. Sitting on
the side-lines was not enough.

---

45. *The New Funk and Wagnalls Encyclopedia*, Vol. 23, p. 8400.
46. *S. & H.* 351:11-15 (Italics mine).

The steps I have taken are intended to reveal more of the Science of Oneness that follows when one leaves behind the dualistic instruction of Christian Science. Living and loving this higher order brings a sustaining harmony, a happier, more total joy, a fresh revelation of one's personal divinity and an appreciative consideration for the divinity of others. It has moved me into a stimulating, more practical experience by relating me to the wholeness of Life. It has brought me to a broader concept of all I survey. Its bounty expands into infinite interpretation.

The inner enlightenment of one's real self reveals the highest realities of Mind, God, Good, as they apply to us in our present earthly realm. We understand our physical structure to be one of *Truth* and *Love* in a divinely personal way, released from the institutional concept of church which kept us very busy unrelentingly "casting out devils, or error . . ." Our questionings are correct for they have forced us out of that activity into the harmony of our divine Being. We may well ask why we should be casting out evils while we are simultaneously taught that in Truth there is no evil to be cast out! Review again the chapter on *The Translation of Animal Magnetism* in *The Bridge* to find out what phantoms you dealt with in the early instruction—figments of imagination that have no place in the higher order of your harmonious Being!

Mrs. Eddy does not hesitate to tell us about her Congregational Church experience: "After a lifetime of orthodoxy on the platform of doctrines, rites, and ceremonies, it became a sacred duty . . . to impart to

others this new-old knowledge of God."[47] She is talking about her discovery of Christian Science. She had
had her fill of tradition. It belonged to the old-time
faith, but ". . . above the frozen crust of creed
and dogma, the divine Mind-force . . . upheaves the
earth."[48] Ponder this statement; consider her thoughts
about ritualism and dogma which ". . ..freeze out the
spiritual element"![49]

We read in *The First Edition of Science and Health*,
pages 166-167: "No time was lost by our Master in
organizations, rites, and ceremonies, or in proselyting
for certain forms of belief: members of his church must
answer to themselves, in the secret sanctuary of Soul,
questions of the most solemn import." At this early date
in Mrs. Eddy's experience she also wrote on the same
page: ". . . a magnificent edifice was not the sign of
Christ's Church." Hugh A. Studdert-Kennedy in his
book, *Christian Science and Organized Religion*, says
that Mrs. Eddy ". . . was obviously determined, in
those early days, not to launch a church, and it was
only when—as the result of repeated setbacks and of
unremitting pressure on the part of her followers—
she concluded, apparently, that organization is an in-
escapable part of the *unenlightened human view of
religion*, that she surrendered to the inevitable and un-
dertook the founding of a Church."[50]

We are all acquainted with the way in which Jesus
silenced his disciples after they had been on the mount

---

47. *No.* 12:9-12
48. *Mis.* 331:22-24
49. *Ret.* 65:7
50. Hugh A. Studdert-Kennedy: *Christian Science and Organized Religion.*
The Farallon Press, Los Gatos, California, 1947. p. 104 (Italics mine).

of transfiguration. The moment after they saw Jesus appearing with Moses and Elijah, Peter thought it would be a great idea to make tabernacles in the name of each of them, but soon after their vision Jesus told Peter, James and John to tell this vision to no man until a later date! He did not wish them to broadcast what they had seen, certainly not to create an organization founded on the import of their amazing experience. Jesus was not born to organize a church, but his message, and the many interpretations given to it, have resulted in the formation of many churches because needs demanded it.

In *The Christian Science Journal* for March 1892, Mrs. Eddy wrote that organizing a material church was dispensable, that it was ". . . not absolutely necessary to ordain pastors and to dedicate churches; but if this be done, let it be in concession to the period, and not as a perpetual or indispensable ceremonial of the Church." This quotation is from Hugh Studdert-Kennedy's book, *Christian Science and Organized Religion*, p. 106.

Now, of course, I write this out because many students have found themselves advanced beyond traditional Christian Science, realizing what was happening in their own church by the freezing process Mrs. Eddy has written about. They became separated from their traditional work with dualism into a higher order of Church where they know they are ". . . The structure of Truth and Love . . ." (*Science and Health*, 583:12). In this they are promoting a personal oneness concept of church which is in itself inspiring.

A serious study by some individuals who have left

the Christian Science organization, other than those mentioned in my previous books, show that in leaving it they experienced a feeling of liberation and harmony *as Science* outside of officialdom. J. Stillson Judah in his book, *The History and Philosophy of The Metaphysical Movements in America* lists a few of them: Emma Curtis Hopkins, Ursula Gestafeld, and Annie C. Bill. He says: "In recent years other noted members have left the church, some of whom rebelled against the strictness of the Christian Science oligarchy in matters of philosophical interpretation."[51]

With my own departure from orthodoxy, I have written *The Bridge, Identity* and now *Harmony of Being* in order to point out to the traditional Christian Scientist that there is a positive principle with which to identify and this is in fact the very Science of Celestial Being. It reveals a more personal and wider discovery of present, livable reality. How many times have we been asked to consider this, from the Bible: "...they that worship *him* must worship *him* in spirit and in truth." Today, as Spirit and Truth, we revere our personal spirituality; we know the place and the importance of our divine heritage, right here in our mortality. The "him" to worship is our very own spiritual withinness. We respect and honor divinity by acknowledging Spirit and Truth as the God-expression of our human lives.

A book entitled, *Finding Your Self*, by W. Norman Cooper, C.S.B., presents this on page 78:

---

51. J. Stillson Judah: *The History and Philosophy of The Metaphysical Movements in America.* Westminster Press, Philadelphia, Pennsylvania, copyright MCMLXVII, page 286, used by permission.

Too frequently Christianity has been so pre-
occupied with its creeds, doctrines, and dogmas that it has been unable to point the way
to God . . . Why? Because they have been
about God. Our search should not be so much
to find out about God as to *be* the God-
power, individually expressed. And being the
God-power, individually expressed, is being
your Self. Sometimes the study of creeds, doctrines, and dogmas has become a substitute
for the search for the God-power within . . .
[This may seem] easier than the inner soul-
searching experience . . . [but of itself it] can
never bring the bliss which comes from the
consecrated searching for and finding the Self
within.[52]

A woman called me to ask if I would speak to a
man who was in a local hospital. Of course I said I
would, and when I called he said he simply wanted
support in the truth he already knew. He had read
The Bridge and had identified with its premise, and
as we talked about the higher order of Science and of
the presence of our God-Being wherever we are and
whatever our condition, I felt his confidence and peace
returning to him. After his release from the hospital
he made an appointment to see me. At this visit he
told me that although he had been a student for over
58 years he never became a member because he could
not accept the organizational doctrine, and he also said

52. W. Norman Cooper, C.S.B.: *Finding Your Self*. DeVorss & Co.,
Marina del Rey, Ca. 90291, copyright 1974.

that the conclusions he had reached from his years of metaphysical study of Christian Science he found fully stated in *The Bridge*. He never did accept the orthodoxy even though his wife had been a member of the church. *The Bridge,* he felt, represented his own spiritual arrival, and in accordance with the premise of Oneness he had accepted his stay in the hospital knowing he was not in any way separated from God. His call to me reinforced his understanding that "God is All," whether one is in a hospital or not in one.

I am introducing him to you now as one who followed out Mrs. Eddy's original plan: to advance individually, spiritually, by applying the rudiments laid down in her textbook, moving through various states and stages of thought according to one's developing spiritual understanding. This man's dedicated work and the natural unfoldment of the Science within Christian Science led him to its higher discovery without church affiliation. I rejoice that he is present today with us, that he arrived at his point of understanding before reading *The Bridge,* and was able to identify with its higher order of Being as *himself!*

It is interesting to note that with the publication of *The First Edition of Science and Health,* the author's expectation was that Christian Science would be promptly accepted in the homes of Christians and from their study of it they would advance according to their receptivity. After all, in the instruction of Christian Science there are beliefs of atonement, the crucifixion, the resurrection, the ascension, probation and salvation. Mrs. Eddy, however, interpreted these subjects metaphysically and this gave her religion a new meaning. She felt there was no need for a specific church to promote Christian Science because her Science, being founded on the Bible, would find its place developing in existing Protestant organizations. It was her hope that the churches of the day would accept her ideas and promote them. She was presenting these *to be incorporated into* Christianity; she was not planning a separate church at all!

———

I am not at all surprised at the number of students who have told me that when they first came into Christian Science they were impressed by the beauty of its positive approach to life. They felt certain that a continued study of it would make all things possible and bring about every solution. After many years of membership, however, questions arose when they began to think more deeply about the content of the Lesson-Sermons and about their personal commitment to the organization. A dualistic form of the teachings became evident. The "All-is-Mind-versus-All-is-not-Mind" dichotomy made them feel uncomfortable, and they longed to get back to their earlier inspiration, to return to the affirmative ideas which drew them to Christian Science in the first place.

All I can say in explanation of these feelings is that many started out with the fact of God's Allness and Love only to find later on that they became mired in the organizational arena surrounded by ideational inconsistencies. There was greater involvement with sub-

ordinate activities which demanded the hoped-for continuing inspiration and revelation. They were instructed
in the handling of error so often that *more work had
to be done in this area than in acknowledging their
original premise that God is All-in-all!* To illustrate
this let me read a letter from one who has just read
Identity. She writes:

> I never forgot . . . what happened once dur-
> ing class instruction. One of the students told
> of the "protection" she had had on several
> occasions. When she finished . . . my teacher,
> a pupil of Mr. Kimball, said, "My dear, in-
> stead of going to all that work, the need was
> to identify yourself correctly and *that is your
> protection!*"

In this case the student had been faithfully following
the orthodox teaching of Christian Science in protect-
ing herself against animal magnetism, whereas the
teacher was leading her out of it through his dedicated
work into the higher order of Science, although he may
not have known this. He knew very well, however, that
there was no need to be concerned about a non-existent
phantom. He gave her not only a higher understanding
of herself as God-everpresent but also a very practical
explanation of the harmony of her being in a new way.
You see, the sooner you get over all the protective work
the way opens for your understanding that God is all
and God is Love and God is the center and circumference of your divinity.

Just before I became a member of the Christian
Science Church, *The Reader's Digest* had asked its

subscribers to write an article on "Why I Go To Church." Christian Science was then the most important thing in my life, so I sat down and wrote my reactions to the services I was attending at Eighth Church in New York City. If I were to read it to you now you would see that it was written completely from the premise of God's Allness and from my sincere desire to relate to that premise. I had not yet become concerned about "protection," the business of annihilation, the dualism, or the animal magnetism that later on would present themselves so insistently in the content of the Lesson-Sermons. While all this instruction had its place and was a natural sequence in my life, something more wonderful happened as I reached for a sustaining harmony. I found it when I became aware that it was essential for me to hold to an absolute Oneness without compromise. This realization is precisely what is taking place in the lives of many students today. It is a glorious advancement which identifies them beautifully with this quotation: "Our surety is in our confidence that we are indeed dwellers . . . [as] Truth and Love, man's eternal mansion. Such a heavenly assurance ends all warfare, and bids tumult cease, for the good fight we have waged is over [through the instruction], and divine Love [the higher order of our divine being] gives us the true sense of victory."[53] It is this divine love that continues sharing the good news—and this love is within us.

---

53. *Pul.* 3:11-15

How satisfied we are when something very signifi-
cant is being shown to us just at the right moment and
in the right place. Its timing and its location encourage
us to identify with it, and in the identification we receive a richness that later we recall as a very high point
in our memory. I had such an experience in Honolulu
several years ago. I was reading a passage from *Science
and Health* which pointed out the beauty of Mount
Zion and the city foursquare. It was at this sentence
that I stopped to rejoice: ". . . southward, to the genial
tropics, with the Southern Cross in the skies . . . west-
ward, to the grand realization of the Golden Shore of
Love and the *Peaceful Sea of Harmony*."[54] For me
these were not merely words in a book; I was having a
spiritual encounter with myself. After all, here I was
actually experiencing these "genial tropics," on "the
Golden Shore of Love," physically enjoying the "peaceful sea of harmony." These words referred to my very
own Being! They came alive to me as a personal-
spiritual awareness of my glorious, present universe and
I responded to them in full measure.

I had another experience a few years later while I
was in Hana, on the Island of Maui, Hawaii. I needed
plumeria flowers to make some leis, and I was given
permission to pick them from a flowering tree near a
cemetery in back of the Congregational Church. As I
gathered them I was inspired to write this poem:

---

54. *S. & H.* 575:29 to 576:2 (Italics mine).

THE LEI

I picked them, every one from
A tree in the old church ground.
  So very beautiful they were
  And warm
From the glowing sun.
As I reached high above Hana's rich earth
  I thought:

Man is not closed within tombs.
Like the ever-returning plumerias
  He is forever alive,
  Now in full splendor,
Marvelously awake to Life's
Renewing form and substance!
  And I knew that

Life is eternal. The circle lies
Within the lei;
  Man and the plumeria,
  Present with us always
In a state of grace and life,
Lovingly sharing the lei.
  Aloha, Hawaii.

On August 27th, 1974, the *Pulekina* arrived from
Hana. It is a weekly newspaper which we have been
receiving since living there for a month when my husband was the resident physician. In it I read that
Charles Lindbergh had died and had chosen to be

buried in Hana, and although this poem was written long before his death, it is fitting that I dedicate it to him at this time.

Today we know that I AM as *us* is ". . . Science, still enthroned . . . unfolding [to us] . . . the immutable, harmonious, divine Principle . . . unfolding *Life* and the universe, ever present and eternal!"[55] Life is the eternal fact which includes birth and death in its universal and forever-renewing, eternal plan. "Man in the likeness of God as revealed in Science cannot help being immortal."[56] This statement is about *you; you* are the man immortal. What we call death is a return to a quiet part of life, a time for renewal and beginning. For life to be eternal it must be in the form of an endless circle and it is in this that death becomes merely a way-station in the great continuity. What joy in knowing your life to be immortal, here forever— changing, renewing forms, but Life always.

All these thoughts that I am presenting simply say that if you are not living your Science every day, if you are not happily identifying with what you know to be the highest image of yourself and are not realizing the Harmony of Being, then you are using a great deal of your precious time without reaping the joyous rewards. The Science of your Celestial Being seen as your living heritage brings you daily blessings, the fulfillment of your faith. It is essential to be daily receptive, to be expectant of the grand potential this heritage has for you. Stay in this harmony always; be grateful for everything. Rejoice!

---

55. *S. & H.* 306:26-29 (Italics mine).
56. *S. & H.* 81:17-18

How should we live each day? Your Scientific understanding informs you. It is as the ". . . irradiance of Life; light, the spiritual idea of Truth and Love."[57] It is in this realm of thought that the harmony of your life expresses itself and this realm is brought to you visibly concrete by your own insistent living as a spiritual idea. Practice this irradiance. See your spiritual needs being met; feel your aspirations as physical counterparts of your Spirit. Go beyond what you can grasp! Reach out! Immortalities are in your glorious mortality each day; it is your mortality that expresses itself as person/place/thing in your world of spirit. William Blake has put this thought into glorious words in his *Auguries of Innocence.*

> To see a World in a grain of sand
> And a Heaven in a wild flower,
> Hold Infinity in the palm of your hand
> And Eternity in an hour.

You are the Mind that ". . . measures time according to the good that is unfolded."[58] This revealed view is God's day, and God's day is each and every one of our days full of the Allness of Spirit, abounding with energy and activated by our inspiration and creativity. Be aware of a constant, grand assurance within you that you are at all times controlled and directed by love. "Hold infinity in the palm of your hand." Accept this harmonious consciousness. Work with abundant joy, give of yourself in every situation, let creative Mind

57. *S. & H.* 584:1-2
58. *S. & H.* 584:6

be your Mind. Know that "The spiritualization of our
sense of man [one's self] opens the gates of paradise . . ."⁵⁹ for you, a place of bliss, a state of happiness here and now and not as an experience we were
told to expect only in the future. Point yourself toward
the high achievement always; do your work joyously
whatever it is as the higher order of your Being. Relate! Identify! Personify! Glorify! Harmonize with your
spiritual Allness!

You see, letting God do it is not enough, if by this
we mean having something outside ourselves be responsible for our lives while we sit back and wait for
results. If we want the best for ourselves we must first
have this expectation and then *we must work for it.*
Through our acceptance of God-power and might as
our power and might we are showing ourselves the
way to fulfillment.

Do you sometimes entertain thoughts of fear or discouragement, of sadness, grief or failure—thoughts of
separation, of loneliness or lack or illness? Remember
it is what you do with these moments that makes all
the difference as to what follows. How do you respond
when such thoughts appear? You can know that such
extremities are your opportunities. In the higher order
of Science you have the divine capacity to rise to the
harmony of being, to receive the spiritual support that
is already within you. Today we ". . . let the harmonious and true sense of Life and being *take possession* of
[our] human consciousness."⁶⁰

---

59. *Mis.* 185:19-20
60. *S. & H.* 355:12-13 (Italics mine).

Here is a letter from my husband, stationed in the Southwest Pacific in World War II, written by him when he received word from me that we had lost our first child in childbirth. The response from him at that time was so wonderful that I feel I must share it with you.

Your letter about the baby received. There is no loss, sweetheart. It is only that our gain in this respect has been postponed until the future. Do not be disappointed or discouraged, for this is an opportunity for us to express in concrete form our knowledge of the truth of our living. Be grateful for all we have, even more than before. I am not hurt by this episode for it cannot be adverse, no matter how difficult it may seem to understand. There is an explanation which will be shown to us. Be calm and confident, peaceful in our unity with each other and with the spirit of love.

The message was sent to me in the Greenwich (Connecticut) Hospital by The American Red Cross. My husband was then working as a physician in an Army field hospital in the jungles of New Guinea. The quality of his attitude in this difficult circumstance is beautifully epitomized in the following poem by Elena Goforth Whitehead. It is one which can benefit all of us, no matter what situations or conditions may be ours.

JOY IS IN ATTITUDE

There is a happiness, mine to possess,
That no event can frustrate or exclude.
It is felicity of consciousness,
The peace and power of chosen attitude.
No episode can gladden or annoy
Without a mood to gauge it and react.
Events cause neither misery nor joy
Til attitude gives value to the fact.
My attitude can drain distress away
And sharpen pleasure to a keen degree
Or, bringing faith and feeling into play,
Can change a fact to meet my certainty.
No joy is too remote to be foretold,
For life enforces attitudes I hold.[61]

John M. Dorsey has something to say about this, too:

The sure immediate cure for every complaint . . . is to give myself another dose of God-consciousness. It is my God-consciousness which turns all apparent badness to goodness, all apparent time to eternity, all seeming space to infinity, all manifest war to peace . . . in short, all seeming devilry to divinity. Of whatever happens I observe, "Something divine has happened."[62]

---

61. Elena Goforth Whitehead:*Attitudes*. Privately Printed. 378 Belmont Street, Oakland, California, 94610, copyright 1973, page 9.
62. John M. Dorsey, M.D.: *Illness or Allness*. Wayne State Univ. Press, Detroit, 1965, p. 478.

Divine Love constantly places us where we are often appreciated as expressions of Life, Truth and Love. We do not keep these qualities hidden; we share what we have. We rejoice with others as their opportunities arrive and the receptive hearts prepare. Oh, yes, *there are others,* and I mean *other persons,* because Mind is infinite in its manifestations, and these *others* are its glorious manifestation made visibly evident in our lives. Let us be grateful for their divinely personal appearances as relatives, as friends, acquaintances, neighbors —for that matter all those we meet. They are part of the heavenly harmony which comprises our objective-subjective experience, our One World, and the story I am now about to relate shows how identity with my universe brought me an opportunity to express some higher order thoughts to someone I had never seen before.

On Mother's day, May 12, 1974, I was walking along Stradella Road with my little dog, Rebel. A short, distance from my home I noticed a young man parked in a car; he was reading the Bible. I walked on, but when I returned I was compelled to stop and say something to him, and it was this: "What a wonderful place to be having your own church service!" He said he was there because he was trying to resolve a problem, and he felt drawn to this quiet atmosphere where he could read portions of his Bible. When I asked him what part of it he found helpful he cited several passages from the New Testament, John. Soon we were in the midst of a discussion on religion. He said that although he attended his church that morning, he had for a long time been aware of a more universal concept of church within himself, and he felt that he belonged to all churches now because he had accepted Jesus as his Saviour.

He asked me for my views. I told him I had outgrown the orthodoxy of my own church and that my liberating thoughts permitted me to experience a more universal concept wherein I was able to see God, Good, everywhere. I gave him a brief history of myself as a Christian Science practitioner, and of having written *The Bridge,* a book my church considered unauthorized and for the writing of which I had been excommunicated. At this point he started reading from the Bible, Matthew 5:11: "Blessed are ye when men shall revile you, and persecute you, and shall say all manner of evil against you falsely for my sake. Rejoice and be exceeding glad: for great is your reward in heaven; for so persecuted they the prophets which were before you." He was lovingly attempting to console me, but I told him I did not feel persecuted in that sense at all. I could not identify with that passage. What I did was what I believed I was spiritually prepared to do, and I told him that because of this work, which I considered a divine direction, I received a wonderful sense of harmony and fulfillment. I also said I fully understood that my church's action toward me was the highest it knew, and I held no adverse judgment.

Our discussion returned to the reason why he found himself on the road doing his prayerful work in the car. Finally he said he felt like telling me about it. He said he was engaged to be married on June 22nd, but on many occasions recently he had been upset with his fiancee about her parents. He frankly admitted he was jealous of the time she spent with them instead of with him. He felt he should be more important to her. I pointed out that his real importance was in the spiritual identification he had made earlier from the passage he read to me from the Bible. He agreed that this was important, BUT . . .

When his fiancee told him she was going to spend the day with her parents, he told her to go on without him. This brought him to Stradella Road. I reminded him that this was Mother's Day, a most special family day, and this was reason enough for her to visit her parents. I suggested that the only possible way to resolve his problem was for him to express the love he was professing that Jesus had had for *his* mankind and to let this same spirit of love be made practical and demonstrated to his fiancee, and to her mother and father as well, by going to the home of his fiancee and expressing it directly. I told him how important it was for him to identify more as *the living Christ,* of whom he spoke with such knowledge and sincerity, and that in this way he would be establishing this identity in his *own* life. Having a great spiritual harmony within himself he should know that in truth there is no jealousy at all! How could there be when to each of us there is only a completeness of love for each other? His receptivity was immediate, and I saw the joy of his Christ-Being illuminate his face.

My gaze wandered to a portrait on the seat of his car. It was a beautiful water-color print of a *smiling* Jesus. I recognized it at once as a print I had seen in *The Los Angeles Times* during the Easter Season. My husband thought it was an exceptionally good drawing, but even more than this he said it was most original in that it depicted Jesus not as a man of great sorrow but a man of joy! What could be more appropriate for

Easter? To my delight and surprise he said he was the artist who made this illustration for his church to advertise their service. I asked him if I could buy the print but he said he would be happy to give it to me. Then, with the assurance of one convinced of his decision, he said: "My problem is solved. I am on my way to my fiancee's home to express the love and peace that is now in my heart." His harmony and radiant joy had returned to him.

Peace and harmony of heart and mind come to us as we resolve situations knowing *we are the love that resolves them.* Having a liveable, conscious awareness of the Christ as your own substance does not mean that your life will necessarily be a bed of roses, but the wonderful part of knowing what and who you really are enables you to make correct and loving decisions about each and every circmumstance. "Divine love always has met and always will meet every human need."[63] This divine love, the Christ consciousness which you are, governs and directs every step of your way. "If you take each day and lift it to the highest you can reach, knowing that each day's problems will be solved spiritually, you will be given almost direct action . . . changing water into wine."[64]

In our metaphysical work in The Higher Order of Science we are ". . . conscious [of] spiritual harmony and eternal being."[65] We identify as New Jerusalem *personally* for it is "Divine Science; the spiritual facts

63. *S. & H.* 494:10-11
64. *Letters of the Scattered Brotherhood,* p. 154. Edited by Mary Strong. Harper and Row, copyright 1948.
65. *S. & H.* 521:2-3

and harmony of the universe, the kingdom of heaven or reign of harmony."[66]

In other words we relate to every person as *Love*, to our universe as *Life*, to religious integrity wherever expressed as *Truth*, to nature and our individuality as *Spirit*, to the order and activity of our being as *Principle*, to our depth of feeling as *Soul*, and to our *Mind* as the consciousness of divinity embracing all in a forever-expanding and glorious unity.

A woman who was converted from her religion to Christian Science wanted to discuss a problem that had arisen in her daughter's family, where the husband's religion was Judaism. Although the daughter had had early instruction in Christian Science she was no longer interested in it, and had decided to send her children to the synagogue for their religious training. Her mother was explaining to me that she did not have anything in common with her grandchildren because of their religious background. I lovingly reassured her that she had a great deal in common with them. She was certainly at one with them in her knowledge of Life, Truth and Love, and she had the Bible with its full and complete revelation of the Old Testament. She could communicate many things from it to her grandchildren and she could learn from them as well. There was in fact no need to feel separate from them at all. Her understanding of Science, when viewed correctly, would bring them closer to her. It was a matter of accepting *all* as *Oneness* in a demonstration of perfect understanding. This healing did not come about at once, but in due time I watched her harmony return as she

---

66. *S. & H.* 592:18-20

grew to understand that the concept of love she knew in Christian Science was really something for everyone. The disunity dissolved and her unhappy concerns vanished.

My husband and I were invited to a Bar Mitzvah. Our friend's son is 13 years old and in this meeting we were introduced to a service which signifies that religious maturity of the son has been reached. In his 13th year he is ready to assume many of the responsibilities of an adult. It is a time for him to express his allegiance to his faith, a time to adopt mature attitudes of social consciousness, a time to review his affection for his family and to begin the development of personal talents as a human being.

We know this young boy and were aware that he had a great potential. In the pamphlet given to the congregation I was interested in this: "Bar Mitzvah is not a revolution in a boy's development; it is a highlight giving extra meaning to the everyday, routine business of growing up." In explaining the significance of this day the Rabbi said the following: "The strength of Judaism consists in this: that as soon as one period in history comes to an end, another begins. A new idea replaces the old, fresh forces come into play, and the result is a continuous progress. The spiritual strength of a young man in modern times is much the same. As soon as one state in his development ends another begins." My husband and I were very touched by this experience. We were happy to participate in this ceremony and to recognize the importance it held for this young man. It was an opportunity for us to see the good appearing for him within the framework of this special instruction.

The Science of Celestial Being restores peace to the body as well as peace to the mind. Let me share this letter with you:

> Just a note to thank you for helping me with the treatments for my back. They were completely effective. After the second treatment I was very much better and after a few days almost completely well. Now I have no difficulty at all. Where before I could not raise my right leg without pain, I can now do it; in fact I can *kick* like a ballet dancer!

A definition of body which coincides with an acceptance of our spiritual habitation is ". . . the superstructure of Truth; the shrine of Love . . ."[67] I referred this metaphysical definition to a woman who felt that her advancing years were giving her a lot of trouble. She started out by telling me that she was denying she had ever been born, denying the fact she was getting older, and denying all the functions of her material body! Of course, this is not uncommon for one who is reared in the instruction of traditional Christian Science. I lovingly advised her to stop all negative work and to start being grateful for the years her wonderful body had served her so well. I gave her

---

67. *S. & H.* 595:8-9

several higher order references on *body* which she could identify with as her own divine body substance. I watched her gratitude dissolve the many arguments she had been using against herself; she began to appreciate the strength and beauty of function characterizing the "incredible machine" which constituted her material form. This brought about the peace and harmony she desired.

In a cartoon I saw recently by Charles Schultz in *The Los Angeles Times* Mary Lou is throwing a ball to Chuck. He misses it, it hits him and he falls to the ground. She is standing over him saying: "Coordination and communication . . . these are your problems, Chuck!" While he is still groggy she continues, "Your mind tells your body to do something, but your body doesn't obey . . . Your mind and body have to work together . . ." Then Chuck sits up and says: "My mind and my body hate each other!" Now is this not typical of traditional Christian Science doctrine where mortal mind and body in this concept are both erroneous and therefore incapable of loving in the real sense? But placed in the higher order of Science, the harmony of being, we understand mind and body to be harmoniously integrated and we love and reverence them as Mind's structural manifestation.

I would like to remind you again: If you take your concordances and study the word *body*, you will find two divergent concepts. In order not to be confused by these different interpretations it is necessary to identify with your higher order of *body*. In the new work we do not deny it; we love it, reverence it, appreciate it and find ourselves consistently grateful for

its substantive expression. We glorify its spiritual substance and its marvelous function!

In a previous paragraph I spoke of "the incredible
machine," the subject of a television program I watched
recently. It was a documentary description of some of
our body's activities. I was able to realize again how
fascinating and remarkable our bodies are, something
I would not have been able to appreciate when I was
in the instruction of orthodox Christian Science. In the
higher order of body (the positive acceptance of it) we
find that there is much advancing work to do in understanding this wonderfully harmonious organism. Use
your concordances to relate *only* to those statements
that raise your consciousness to the high values where
body is your temple, your spiritual habitation. I feel
confident that any problem you have with body will be
helped if you praise, bless, and glorify rather than
deny, annihilate, deprecate and ignore.

As mentioned in *The Bridge,* I have a folder in my
files containing letters from those who have experienced
healing after having been supported in spiritual understanding. The practice of Christian Science healing is
the practice of love and harmony. We may call it many
different things: Holy Ghost, Spirit, God, Christ-consciousness, illumination, but whatever, the name *love*
fits them all. "If the Scientist reaches his patient
through divine Love, the healing work will be accom-
plished at one visit . . ."[68] Accepting love we accept
harmony. Practice is a loving reminder to the body that
our Harmony of Being is our normal physical/spiritual
state of consciousness and the degree of our sincerity

---

68. *S. & H.* 365:15-17

in accepting this knowledge for ourselves determines
the immediacy of a response to our requests. Marcus
Aurelius said, "All that is harmony for thee, O universe, is in harmony with me as well."

Class notes on *Identity* contain the following:

> We understand Principle in such a way that
> our work as metaphysicians is a joy. There is
> no need for an advanced student to go
> through a lot of metaphysical arguing (with
> "erroneous claims"). To be sure, this method
> had its day (within the instruction) and we
> are grateful for the good received from it,
> but it is not needed by us now.[69]

We hold to our harmony of being (heavenly state
of consciousness) in every circumstance and situation,
recalling that whatever is going on is the divine revelation unfolding for us and within us, Principle and love
at work. There is no guilt, no condemnation; there is
only love keeping us courageously knowing the truth
about ourselves to ourselves.

I enjoyed reading this letter from one who was
telling me how she was working out her harmony of
love with her family. She writes:

> Your books have been very helpful to me in
> seeing that the mortality of the members of
> my family is their divinity, that whatever they
> are doing is *their highest sense of good and*

---

69. Irene S. Moore, C.S.: *Identity,* page 62, DeVorss & Co., Marina del
Rey, Ca. 90291, copyright 1974.

love for now, and that they are Spirit and divine here and now in the flesh. How love is working out its purpose doesn't seem always to be apparent, but your books have been helping me more to see that all this isn't a terrible thing that has happened but that there is a blessing in it for all of us.

Now isn't this a wonderful way to put into practice the Harmony of Being! It benefits her as well as those she loves!

———

On August 14, 1922, Bicknell Young, C.S.B., in addressing a class, had this to say:

You will find in studying Mrs. Eddy's works, there is something there to be unfolded far greater than has been perceived, and something to be demonstrated that has never been shown forth. We have the right to expect *that we will go beyond to greater unfoldments, gaining heights not previously attained.*

I sincerely feel that The Higher Order of Science within Christian Science *is* this greater unfoldment.

Mrs. Lucia Coulson was reported to have told her companion, Ruby Grant, something which Mrs. Eddy said to Laura Sargeant, a worker in her home, about the final edition of *Science and Health.* In responding to a question Mrs. Eddy said:

There, Laura, I have put my discovery out
into mortal mind, and I have hidden it, and
hidden it, and hidden it, and if I hide it anymore, my discovery will be lost.

When this story was given to me I immediately
thought that raising mortal mind into its state of immortality for each and everyone of us could be the
hidden discovery she was referring to. By taking Christian Science out of the dualism of its primary instruction and raising it to the Oneness concept, we reach
The Higher Order of Science which we find today *is
the discovery*. Only with this higher understanding can
we relate consciously to the wonderful identification
where ". . . God is harmony's selfhood,"[70] knowing it
to be ourselves. This is the enlightening effect of a
fresh discovery. We say nothing is impossible to God.
Then doesn't it follow that nothing is impossible to us
and that Man is ". . . harmony's selfhood"? This identification is a most strengthening acknowledgment, co-
inciding with the concept we hold of ourselves as
Harmony, God-Being *us*. Receive this as your personal-
spiritual habitation where you live and breathe and
glorify your harmony of being *unconditionally*. Mrs.
Eddy tells us that attaining these divine conceptions
of immortality makes up the only true concept of being.
This understanding of ourselves is reached in our mortal state because it is a mental/spiritual concept. I have
paraphrased this from the marginal heading "spiritual
discovery."[71]

---

70. *Un.* 13:8-9
71. *S. & H.* 260:8-12

After reading my books Rozella Rush wrote:

> I certainly don't want to belittle mortality
> anymore. I feel that Christian Science often
> sounds so abstract that your approach to it
> brings it into the everyday realm of life, into
> more practical application, one's own divine,
> everyday living . . . I am delighted to read
> how you stress our divinity here and now in
> the flesh, and I mean stress it. I kept saying
> to myself, *right, right* . . . It was so reassuring
> to me that I personally am not separate from
> my divinity, that . . . my mind is divine here
> and now as I live my everyday life. And while
> I have been saying I'm my own authority,
> it becomes more clear to me that my divine
> mind *is* its own authority. How else do divine
> thoughts come except to the divine person?
> My mind as I go around in the flesh *is* the all-
> knowing mind. What other mind is there?

The same person has written a wonderful article
entitled *Mortal/Immortal Now* in a periodical called
INSIGHTS, Volume 7, Number 1, April/May 1975.
It is so good that I would like to read it in its entirety,
but right now I am happy to share part of it. Listen
to this:

> We don't try to get rid of a mortal *because
> our Divinity* or Wholeness *includes or is our
> Mortality.* We want to see that our mortality
> is also our immortality, our infinitude, our
> Allness of Mind and Soul. We are the di-

vine world we, as mortals, walk through, and
we are also the divine mortals that do the
walking.

All the experiences of Mind have had purpose
and meaning, no matter if we have thought of
them as unpleasant or wrong. It is our divinity
pointing the way to a fuller and more complete view of ourselves as the divine mortal-
immortal allness of Life and Mind. It has *all*
been part of our divinity experience so we
can't say it doesn't or didn't really exist.
Everything that has happened to us as persons has existed, but our divinity is ever pointing out new ways in which to walk. The
mortal past, present and future is the evolu-
tion of Consciousness, *my* Consciousness.

"Existence, separate from divinity, Science
explains as impossible,"[72] so the divine I that
I am is the mortal/immortal I. No doing
away with persons because that would be trying to do away with forms of Mind, but in
seeing that ". . . spiritual consciousness can
form nothing unlike itself, Spirit . . ."[73] we
find mortal man is spiritual man.

The ever-unfolding Nowness of us in the flesh
is the joy of living. No waiting for tomorrow
to become more spiritual and therefore

72. *S. & H.* 522:10-11
73. *Un.* 35:24-25

> healthier, wealthier, happier. Mortal/im-
> mortal Spirit can't be any more full and com-
> plete than Now. Now is the accepted time;
> Now are the fields white with harvest; *Now*
> are all the living persons, places and things,
> the things of joy and Spirit.

There is no question about this writer having crossed her bridge. She has personally identified as her spiritual self, and I rejoice. Her article is expressing the higher order of Science without calling it that; it arises from her mount of revelation. Great with blessing, I share it with you, coming from another who is writing from the higher plane of her spiritual Oneness.

A friend once said to an author, "Why do you write? Everything you say has been said before, and often better said." And the author replied, "Yes, that is true, to some extent at least, of most of those who write or speak, but *each one says it differently,* and therein lies its value." We welcome diversity; we see it as infinite mind expressed. We "Let the Word have free course and be glorified."[74]

Many years ago I took a course in *General Semantics* taught by J. Samuel Bois, Ph.D. Because of his interest in *The Bridge,* I sent him *Identity* after which he sent me the following letter, and I feel it is important enough to read to you.

> I thank you very much for your gift of a
> copy of *Identity*. You give your own version
> in a beautiful language of the message that

---

74. *No.* 45:24

has echoed from generation to generation within the walls of human abode on this planet saying we are Gods, coalescing into a one God, who is still in the process of being born. There is only one book containing such a message that Korsybski took the liberty to recommend. It is *What is Life?* by Erwin Schrodinger, Nobel-prize physicist!

I was curious to find out about Erwin Schrodinger and I found some reference to him in a book I want to recommend to you for further exploration: *The Ascent of Man,* by J. Bronowski. There will be more about this book later. Alfred Korsybski, mentioned in the quote from Dr. Bois' letter is the author of *Science and Sanity, An Introduction to Non-Aristotelian Systems and General Semantics.*

On October 8th, 1974, Lillian Gish was interviewed by James Day on television. In radiating her customary sweetness and light, she showed an unusual serenity coupled with such a sense of joy that I knew it must all be part of her inner harmony. As the questions were given she replied that whatever came to her had required hard work and perseverance because growing up as a child actress in her day was not by any means a simple matter. It was necessary to discipline herself in order to accomplish anything at all, and in this, among other things, she learned the need to be considerate of others, an action which she termed love.

She was questioned about many subjects. Was she discouraged with present-day events? No, not at all. She saw great progress for the world whether events seemed discouraging or not, and she stated that all people as well as nations were being blessed anyway, if they but had the perception to see it. Did she have a feeling in her meetings with young people that there was a generation gap in her life? How could she? She was out among students in many universities, giving lectures and making contacts with them personally, getting to know them better, and in this she was closer to them. She was only aware of the contributions they were making and she felt that we have as many things to learn from them as they have to learn from us. Was she concerned about *anything?* No, not particularly, although she believed the theatres and movies today were attempting to shock the audiences too much (she spoke of *The Exorcist* as one of the examples), and she said that in her day the movies were much warmer and more sentimental. Pictures in her time could be enjoyed by the entire family, whereas this would not necessarily be true today. She quickly added, however, that she believed all of it to be merely a transitional period in the cinema world and that ultimately she expected something fine to emerge.

The young people, she felt, were going through a period of searching and evaluation, and she saw this as a development and growth which may require considerable patience on our part as we watch the progress. It was inspirational to hear her interesting views. She stated that her life continues to be satisfying, and in looking back she can see her most trying times as opportunities—blessings in disguise. This account of her

interview I share with you because I feel it represents
one who is expressing the harmony of being. Her form
of love expression is but one of the many paths to
harmony.

Celestial harmony holds us firmly in an atmosphere
which shows us things as they really are in form and
substance, and seeing them this way is seeing the essence of Spirit. As students of Christian Science you
may have heard a wonderful story told by my teacher
about his teacher, Bicknell Young. He was fond of
horseback riding and one day, while on a ride with
some of his friends, he suddenly stopped the group and,
looking at a view of spectacular beauty, said, "Isn't
this wonderful; this is my body!" We were told that this
announcement from Bicknell Young meant he knew he
was the full embodiment of all that his soul senses beheld, a practical, personal experience of the Science of
Celestial Being. Later these ideas of reality became
more fully understood and made plain in the higher
order of Science, which students often termed the absolute or Divine Science. There was no need for Bicknell Young to get starry-eyed and go off into a lot of
abstractions by trying to absent himself from his body
in order to feel the spirituality of his universe. He felt
it with all that his five physical senses could portray
because he knew them to be spirit.

Spirituality in all its structural substance is a fundamental part of everyday living and is made evident
wherever one may be and in whatever he is doing.
Every action and every reaction in your life here on

earth is Spirit expressed in everyday human terms. In
the question, "What is Man?" on page 475 of *Science
and Health,* we learn that "He is the compound idea of
God, including all right ideas . . . that which has no
separate mind from God . . ." Is this anyone but *us?*

From our Oneness, from the higher order of Science
which constitutes the harmony of our being, comes a
marvelous truth as us, and I invite you now to accept
it for yourself. "In divine Science, the universe, including man, is spiritual, harmonious, and eternal."[75]
The instruction of Christian Science exposed you to it,
perhaps for the first time; the Higher Order of your
Science expects you to know it is so *NOW.* These wonderful, freeing, illuminating, spiritual discoveries about
ourselves and our universe should be occurring to us all
the time. A woman visited my home on Stradella Road,
and while looking out over the magnificent view of the
city, she exclaimed, "Oh! No wonder you were inspired to write *The Bridge!*" I was happy to inform
her it was not written here; it was written in an apartment in Westwood. I pointed to the hills I had seen
from my Westwood apartment and then showed her
that although I was now looking at the same hills from
another vantage point, in both places my higher order
of harmony existed.

As Christian Science students we have been very
privileged to identify with a Lesson-Sermon called *Reality.* Its sole purpose is to introduce us to the consciousness of God-Substance within us, objectified and sub-
jectified as our Being. Although the lessons allowed us
only hints, glimpses and promises of things to come,

---

75. *S. & H.* 114:27-29

there were many references to pure Spirit that was to be found in them. We were told that these glorious statements about Reality (which are emphasized in my books) were only a foretaste of absolute Christian Science. Its prediction was made a hundred years ago. We know these references to be the higher order of Science within Christian Science and the only reason students do not accept them as their personal Reality of Being is that they have not accepted absolute Christian Science as *a present verity*.

Since my books have been published I have had opportunities to meet many more Christian Scientists, and I have come to realize that not even the instruction of orthodox Christian Science is understood by some of them! Their highest thought seems to be in following its doctrinal direction by rote without attempting to identify spiritually with the meanings in the basic teachings even when they touch upon positive attitudes. Others are oblivious of a need for continual unfoldment or revelation. I do not mean to criticize for surely each is living the highest he knows, but I have made these observations from the conversations I have had with students whom I have interviewed for my classes. The subject of reality in particular is one that is often unclear to them. From our *advanced* work we know that an absolute consciousness of good is within us now, that our lives are of necessity ". . . governed by reality in order to be in harmony with God . . ."[76] and that we know reality to be ". . . spiritual, harmonious, and eternal."[77] But this is also a part of the elementary

76. *S. & H.* 131:4-5
77. *S. & H.* 88:14

teaching. Even beginners should be aware that the reality of their Being is exactly where they are every moment, and then should proceed to an elaboration of this as it applies to their lives.

While Mrs. Eddy's higher concepts and directions are wonderful when totally accepted, there are other writings which also voice a higher order of Science. At this time I wish to introduce you to *Reality Therapy: A New Approach to Psychiatry,* by William Glasser, M.D. This book was sent to me by a liberated Christian Science student. She pointed out several interesting statements giving support to her conception of herself as divine Oneness, seeing also a developing sense of relationship to *her real world.* She decided she was not going to deny her material universe anymore because it did not make sense to throw it way. She now knows it to be an essential and harmonious part of her mortal/immortal existence. She quoted from pages 6 and 7:

> Therapy will be successful when [people] are able to give up denying the world and recognize that reality not only exists but that they must fulfill their needs within its framework. . . . the therapist must not only be able to help the patient accept the real world, but he must then further help him fulfill his needs in the real world so that he will have no inclination in the future to deny its existence.[77½]

[77½]. Glasser, William. M.D.: *Reality Therapy.* Harper & Row, Publishers, Inc. Copyright 1965.

And on pages xiv and xv,

> ... all therapy ... [must be directed] toward
> [the development of a] greater maturity, con-
> scientiousness, responsibility ... Reality Ther-
> apy is not something which should be the ex-
> clusive preoccupation or "property" of a few
> highly trained ... specialists ... It is ... ap-
> propriate ... [for] *everyone*, for its precepts
> and principles are the foundation of success-
> ful, satisfying, social life everywhere.

These are interesting quotations and they fit very
well into what I have been saying in this class, but
perhaps the most important achievement for the woman who sent me this book is that she is now free to
read *many* books, and on different subjects, an interest
which she said was previously closed to her forever
because of the limitations placed upon her as a student
of orthodox Christian Science.

Dr. Glasser wrote especially well on the need to be
loved as well as to love. As students in the instruction
of Christian Science we did not pay a great deal of attention to these needs and, of course, we denied the
reality of persons as well as our material universe because we were taught in many ways that the senses
which perceived these were unreal. What is pointed
out to us in this book as reality is something we were
unable to accept in Christian Science. What we were
supposed to recognize was so spiritual and non-ma-
terial that it was indescribable! So, the result was that
we had neither a material universe *nor* the grand reality! We thought mostly of the spiritual reality to

come! Now we know that in the Harmony of our Being reality is our very own self-substance existing in this present life, and that our acceptance of love as well as the giving of it is the normal and natural way to live our divine existence.

Just let me show you how the dictionary defines this subject: *"Reality*: The fact of being real, someone real or something real, an actual *person,* event or situation. That which has *objective existence* and is not merely an idea. That which is *absolute* or self-existent." This definition surely is one to identify with in the enjoyment of your life where you are today.

May I remind you again: your mortality acquaints you with your immortality, and without your mortality you could never experience your eternal and immortal life here in the flesh. Therefore, in your mortality you fully understand and accept that ". . . spiritual reality is the scientific fact in all things. The spiritual fact, repeated in the action of man [that means you] and the whole universe, *is* harmonious and *is* the ideal of Truth."[78] When we read, "Become conscious for a single moment that life and intelligence are purely spiritual . . ,"[79] go beyond holding it consciously "for a single moment"—hold it forever. I am sure now you see how the instruction of Christian Science was all meant to lead you to the exalted plane that I am presenting in my works.

I would like you to take your concordances sometime and look up all the *higher order statements* on real, realism, reality, realization and realize. Make an in-

---

78. *S. & H.* 207:27-29 (Italics mine).
79. *S. & H.* 14:12-13

teresting observation with yourself. Watch the choices you prefer in these statements; they will indicate the degree of your advancement in Christian Science. As you identify with these you find positive approaches to your lives. You experience greater understanding of what is meant by *Self-realization* and *Self-consciousness*. Make these your own. Live them. Put them into daily practice. Again may I say that "... our lives must be governed by reality in order to be in harmony with God, the divine Principle of all being."[80] We also read in *Science and Health,* 477:26-29: "The Indians caught some glimpses of the underlying reality, when they called a certain beautiful lake 'the smile of the Great Spirit'." Well, they were surely catching more than glimpses; they were recognizing their soul senses combined in an artistic harmony of nature, in no way separate from the beauty and truth of their own Spirit.

Reality is seeing things as they really are, in their present wholeness, their actuality, their authentic beauty of form and outline. Winston Churchill once said he never knew a leaf until he started to draw one. His drawing gave him an intimate awareness of it. In the instruction when we looked at a beautiful lake or a sunset our perception of it was clouded because we considered it a view of matter, therefore not real and always erroneous regardless how lovely it was. We were told that our eyes, being mortal, could not see the *spiritual idea* of reality.

For a moment let us consider what Mrs. Eddy states in her chapter on *Science of Being.* You will recognize this as part of the instruction but not the whole of it,

---

80. *S. & H.* 131:3-5

for the whole of it is to pursue your Science further, going through the obvious dualism to the clarity of its Oneness. Listen to this: *"Nothing* we can say or believe regarding matter is immortal, for matter is temporal and is therefore a mortal phenomenon, a human concept, sometimes beautiful, always erroneous."[81] Now, as a member, if you do not accept this statement, as well as many other negative ones about your self and your universe, you are not considered a loyal Christian Scientist. Within the instruction of Christian Science this statement is a cornerstone of Truth and a loyal member must not question it. If, on the other hand, you *do* question it, perhaps it means you are crossing your bridge and are entering into the higher order of your Science without realizing it. In our higher order of Matter, *which we know to be Spirit,* we see all the glory and its full promise appearing now, and as consciousness we are vital and very much alive to all the beauty around us. This is heaven, harmony, the divine kingdom, the divine beauty, the reality that is.

I met a neighbor one morning as I was coming out of my Lindbrook apartment in Westwood. He was just leaving for the day and his wife at the door was bidding him goodbye. He turned my attention to her, saying, "There is my child." I said good morning to her and after we exchanged a few words I left and went on with my activities. Later that morning I wrote this poem:

---

81. *S. & H.* 277:29-32 (Italics mine).

THERE IS MY CHILD

With a few words that meant so much
He said, "There is my child."
Within moments he was gone
And I was left to look
Upon his child.

The door was open and
Greeting me I saw his wife.
The innocence of his youth was there,
The warmth and generosity
Of his spirit,
The joy and laughter
Of his years,
The graciousness and nobility
Of his world.

There was his child!
The jewel of his life,
The courage of his manhood,
The strength of his being,
The companionship of his soul—
La Dessa.

This man was a writer and several days later I had
an opportunity to show him the poem I had written
about his wife, La Dessa. "Well," he said, "I certainly
thank you for writing it—and it *really is* the truth
about her. All the qualities you have seen in her have
been my greatest blessings, but on the morning when I

made that remark, I did it with tongue-in-cheek because she was drunk."

He said he wondered how she could possibly have given me such a wonderful impression when she was in that state. I had no answer other than that any description of her was the way I had seen her: wholesome, serene and beautiful. I was not giving her a metaphysical treatment; I was not unseeing her drunkenness. I simply saw her beautiful, which is what she was.

There is something special I would like you to understand here. In the traditional instruction we had to face what we termed the *unreality* of a situation and then do our work placing *reality* where we thought the unreality was. In the harmony of being we don't recognize any unreality at all; we hold firmly to the one thing continually going on: Mind's perfection. This is the reality you are in touch with and having it constantly as your consciousness you see situations and conditions that are harmonious and beautiful. Accept this harmony as a condition of your life! Accept your consciousness as completely spiritual and look out upon your universe; glorify its greatness!

Someone defined "ego" as the "I," the "self," the "person," that is, "the organizing, self-preserving, self-expressing component, serving to maintain, liberate, operate, regulate, interpret and protect the ongoing physical, mental and emotional states." We recognize this as ourselves, expecting the harmony of being everywhere. We do not fight, resist, "unsee" or argue. We simply *see the blessing in every action, reaction, over-action—even in inaction*—knowing that "All things work together for good."

One of the statements in *Science and Health* that has required *translation* for me in order to maintain my understanding of Oneness is found on page 554. "There is no such thing as mortality, nor are there . . . mortal beings, because being is immortal, like Deity,— or, rather, being and Deity are inseparable." Can you find mortal existence in this explanation? If you endorse this quotation from Mary Baker Eddy you are accepting whatever you call your being as immortal. Are you ready to accept this? In orthodox Christian Science your physical being is not immortal at all, but in the higher order of your Celestial Being it is, for in this exalted plane whatever may be called mortality *is* your immortality and neither one is separate from Deity. It took a long time for me to learn how to evaluate this in terms of the higher order of Science, but it became clear that if we wish to keep the interpretation in tune with the harmony of our being it is necessary to eliminate the first part of the quotation stated above altogether, and then agree to the second wherein we identify and accept ". . . [our] being . . . [as] immortal, like Deity because [our] being and [our] Deity are inseparable." This is an example of translation— extracting the higher meaning from what is at first a mixture of two different ones. Remember there is nothing wrong about being "like" the divine. Let the divine be divine and we also. Being "like" the divine just means we accept another's identification as our own.

My premise states clearly that mortal/immortal Being is One! So do not hesitate to acknowledge your eternal God-Being in and as your mortality. Holding to this spiritual estimate of yourself is a high point in sustaining your harmony of Being. You will never fear to experience what is called death because you know that now you are immortal even before any such event occurs. Your harmony of life remains indestructible and you continue to rejoice in this spiritual fact regarding yourself. "Christ presents the indestructible man, whom Spirit creates, constitutes, and governs."[82] You are the Christ, the creation of Spirit.

You see you can't say there isn't any mortality because there obviously *is;* this same mortality is the very form of your immortality and if you accept the premise of Oneness it is the universality of it all that is inseparable from deity. Remember: The alternatives to the premise of Oneness are premises of nothingness or of twoness, and neither one of these alternatives will get us anywhere. In my book on *Identity* this is precisely what I show: that the totality of *your* Being is God. Study again the definition of God in *Science and Health* and say "That's me; that is what I AM!" You are synonymous with the definition. You define and form it. Accept this. If you cannot do it perhaps you are still caught in the dualism of traditional Christian Science instruction and you have not yet permitted yourself to rise to the higher order within this very instruction. Your continued work, however, should lead you ultimately to your Divine Oneness. This is the sole purpose of your study.

Let us consider our senses for a moment; just think about them. Your divine taste is so wonderful that you can discriminate everything from soup to nuts, fruits, vegetables and beverages and more. Glorify it. Your hands are beautifully sensitive with the ability to bring

---

82. *S. & H.* 316:20-21

you the quality of warm objects as well as cold, of wood, paper, fabrics, a ribbon, a twig, almost any texture you can possibly conceive, the touch of a flower, or of people. Soul feels. Glorify soul. Eyes tell you differences in color, distance, perspective, space, sky, mountains, earth, trees, lakes, people, buildings and oh, so much more. Glorify vision. Do not say it is "just consciousness" as though it were an abstract experience; know how concrete, real, wonderful, touchable, seeable, feelable are these soul senses which we are and glorify them all.

I love the word "glorify." One of its definitions is: "To make glorious by bestowing glory upon; especially to elevate to celestial glory. To shed radiance or splendor on. To make glorious by presentation in a favorable aspect; as to *glorify* everyday life."

One of my earliest remembrances of glorified consciousness occurred when I was seven years old. I was sitting in a classroom when suddenly, without any reasonable explanation, I became acutely aware of the wonderful functioning of my eyes. I was asking myself how I could see so much with only these tiny little holes to look out of! I watched my teacher and the others in the classroom. Then I let my eyes turn to the window. I saw the sky, the buildings, and for some inexplicable reason I was amazed at how far-seeing and near-seeing focused so clearly. I distinctly remember a bowl of fish that was on the window sill. How small these little fish were, I thought, and how remarkable that at one moment I could see these tiny things swimming in a bowl of water and then in the next include the vastness of the sky!

Later in my life when I became acquainted with the
Bible the words of *Psalm* 139:14 affected me strongly:
"I am fearfully and wonderfully made," and we know
that the word "fearfully" means "reverently." It was
not only this reverence for life but its very tangibility
that impressed me. The advanced Christian Scientist
joyously knows he has ideals that are ". . . indestructible
and glorious . . . real and eternal because [they are]
drawn from Truth [himself] . . ."[83] Rightly estimating
what is real permits him to glorify his soul senses now,
rejoicing in the harmony these bring. Scriabin said:

The Universe resounds with the joyful cry—
I AM!

Oh, how infinite and marvelous is this state of mortality which is given us to glorify. The harmony found
within the higher order of Science presents all these
things to us. *Life* is this highest concept of Self-Soul-
Sense, *your* Self, your deified mortality. Don't we in-
corporate in us all the attributes of Godliness? Then
let us express them *in our present form* as Life, Truth,
Love, Principle, Mind, Soul and Spirit, *substance* and
intelligence. In order to demonstrate them we need
a vehicle of some kind and this vehicle is called "matter." Without it these attributes cannot be recognized.
Surely Life, Truth and Love deserve visible, concrete
form. What would be their value to us here on earth
if they had no physical structure?

Now if the Higher Order of Christian Science is too
absolute for you at this time, then *at least* be "The

---

83. *S. & H.* 359:31 to 360:2

Scientific man in Christian Science . . . [who] sees his
mortality as a loving support to his life while he is
making a sincere effort to understand himself as
Spirit."[84] In the higher order of ourselves we accept
this statement on page 264 of *Science and Health*, line
20: "Spirit and its formations are the only realities of
being." We accept ourselves as Spirit which we now
know to be our material formation or structure. In any
case *glorify* your mortality for the presence of life it so
realistically presents. Continue your study of the higher
order of it and you will find doors opening for you
that reveal more and more of your present Celestial
Being.

At about 2:30 one morning a woman called me
about her little girl who had an earache. After talking
with the mother for a while I asked to talk with the
child. She was crying, and I began at once to tell her
how wonderful her ears were and that perhaps she
could tell me something about them for which she was
grateful. The first thing she said was that she could
hear her footsteps; then she mentioned her mother's
voice, and went on to enumerate many other sounds
she heard. As she talked about them her crying ceased.
I spent more time reminding her how wonderful her
ears were, and I told her to keep her thought on gratitude for them and to remember to bless them. Then
I told her that as she thought all these good things

---

84. Irene S. Moore, C.S.: *The Bridge*, p. 257. DeVorss & Company, 1046
Princeton Drive, Marina del Rey, California, Copyright 1971.

about them she would go to sleep. Her mother reported that soon she did go to sleep in comfort.

The mother of the child is present in this class. How she discovered *The Bridge* (my first book on The Higher Order of Science) in a store window is most interesting, and I would like to share it with you. She said she had been visiting a psychiatrist in Santa Monica and one of the things she told him was of a dream that kept recurring night after night. In it she would come to a bridge and then would be confused as to whether or not to cross it. She mentioned this to him several times during the visits she had with him, but its explanation remained unclear. One day she walked down 4th street in Santa Monica and stopped to look in a window at the Carlton Book Shop. She saw a book in the showcase titled *The Bridge* and, recalling her dreams, she went in and bought it. Soon after she read it she called to tell me her story.

She had been brought up in Christian Science but had long questioned the dualism in its teaching, and of course this brought her many guilt feelings which in turn gave her suggestions that she was being disloyal. Often she condemned herself, feeling that she had departed from the doctrinal platform, but nevertheless the rationality of her questions continued and her honest search for answers did not abate. Finally she accepted the fact that she had reached the point where she felt impelled to make a more serious identification as Self and that she could not do it within the context of orthodoxy. It was at this point that she found *The Bridge*. One can understand her happiness, because it supported her advancing ideas and helped to explain some of her confusion with the traditional instruction.

And I must add here that going to the psychiatrist was part of her soul-searching. It, too, was good because goodness is all there is in the Celestial World we live in. (This woman addressed the class and told us how she now identifies with her Science).

Again may I say that the way one works in the higher order of Science differs very much from how he approaches a situation in the orthodox teaching. In traditional Christian Science our material senses must be denied because we are told they are illusory, unreal, part of a great misconception. In the higher order of that same Science we glorify our senses, magnify the good that is our reality ever-present because the Allness of Good is what we are! Surely you remember we *are* the infinite Mind and its infinite manifestation! Mrs. Eddy's great statement about the Allness of Mind does not exclude us from its plan! We are that Allness! We understand the meaning of this statement in *Science and Health* on page 353, line 16: "All the real is eternal." In the harmony of being we live our reality now.

On page 62 and 63 of *Identity* we read how a woman rose magnificently as the higher order of her eternal, infinite being after reading page 179 of *The Bridge* about "the microscope of Spirit." She wrote:

> Apparently my intuition to see, to *be* Soul awareness, is in agreement with your words. I have had to acknowledge I have a body,— Mind, body, Soul in harmony, right now, right here in this Self-existence *I am!* . . . According to the dictionary "infinite" means "Majestic Wholeness"; isn't that great! The majestic wholeness the allness of Mind is, and its

manifestation being me, as me and for me.
Amen! And it is very good.

I have no hesitation in telling you that the woman
who wrote this to me had been a registered Christian
Science practitioner. You can easily see from this letter that her words and feelings are now those of Mind
itself, the Oneness that she understands as her Self.
Here is positive and blissful approval of harmony expressed as her body, the Oneness concept unified in a
personal definition. I find it most interesting when unity
is connected with the thought of harmony. It is this Oneness that is continually expressing what we see, hear,
feel, taste and know so concretely as our very own unified identity.

In the *First Edition of Science and Health*, page 229:
15-18, read, pause and appreciate the full import of this
reference: "That man epitomizes the universe, and is
the body of God, is apparent to me not only from the
logic of Truth, but in the phenomenon, that is *sometimes* before my spiritual senses . . ." (Italics mine).
This is a marvelous acknowledgment for Mrs. Eddy to
make. Would that this were accepted today as the bed-
rock of Christian Science thought! It appeals to me
very much because I interpret the term "man" as our
present being, and I believe she may have felt the same
way at the moment of her writing it. Having the fullness of her discovery we may well agree with it because
our spiritual senses accept the logic of Truth as our own
being. Every student knows, however, that while many
such absolute, higher order statements are found in this
early edition of *Science and Health,* the edition in use
today emphasizes more relative ideas. Fortunately we

have a choice, but those who continue in the membership must accept what is offered in her later editions or be considered disloyal. Lillian de Waters once told me that she was so considered for having displayed a preference for the *First Edition of Science and Health.*

We read that harmony is heaven and that Science reveals this harmony. Moreover you understand this harmony insofar as it ". . . produces a growing affection for all good . . ." (*Mis.* 337:17-18). Ask yourself a few pertinent questions. Are you knowing each day that you are the Science of Celestial Being? Are you living it? Are you loving it? Are you seeing God, good, in *every* situation and condition? I am sure you have read many times the following definition of *New Jerusalem* in the *Glossary*: "Divine Science; the spiritual facts and harmony of the universe; the kingdom of heaven, or reign of harmony."[85] Have you accepted this as having something to do with you, or have you thought of it as referring to a kind of new location to be reached sometime in the hereafter? Remember that this statement is describing ". . . the spiritual outpouring of bliss and glory . . ."[86] which exists as a high state of consciousness *here* and *now* for us to enjoy. We read that "This heavenly city . . . this New Jerusalem, this infinite All . . . reached St. John's vision *while yet he tabernacled with mortals.*"[87] He was with people like you and me when he reached revelation's summit, and he was mortal himself while he was envisioning this heavenly city. We talked about this city earlier. *It is not hidden* from our scientific consciousness because we have accepted the

85. *S. & H.* 592:18-20
86. *S. & H.* 574:14-15
87. *S. & H.* 576:3-7 (Italics mine).

spiritual fact of our universe. This New Jerusalem is our inherent being, our spiritual habitation in the flesh that is included in our acceptance of the great statement that "All is infinite Mind and its infinite manifestation, for God is *All-in-all*."[88] Please stop here to think more about this statement than you ever have before. Notice the "All-in-all," and come to the grand conclusions, with the capital A and the small a.

The Celebration of Life is a most profound book. It is written by Norman Cousins and I should like to refer you to some of its contents. We read: ". . . nothing about human life is more precious than that we can define our own purpose and shape our own destiny."[89] To the question, "Do you have a definition of human purpose you would have me consider?", the answer is:

I would have you consider that the highest purpose of the human species is to justify the gift of life. We do this in many ways: by being aware of its preciousness . . . by developing to the fullest the potentialities and sensitivities that come with life; by putting the whole of our intelligence to work in sustaining and enhancing the conditions that make life possible; by cherishing the human habitat and shielding it from devastation and depletion; by

---

88. *S. & H.* 468:10-11 (Italics mine).
89. Norman Cousins: *The Celebration of Life: A Dialogue On Immortality And Infinity.* Harper & Row, Publishers, New York, Copyright, 1974, pages 68, 69, 82 and 83.

using our free will to the utmost in advancing
the cause of life; finally, by celebrating life.[89]

In describing one of his articles of faith, among the
many, he says, "I glory in the individuality of self, but
my individuality does not separate me from my universal self—the oneness of man."[89]

Reverence for life is more than solicitude or
sensitivity for life. It is a sense of the whole,
a capacity for inspired response, a respect for
the intricate universe of individual life. It is
the supreme awareness of awareness itself.[89]

All these statements represent to me the higher order
of Myself. I hope you realize by now that the references
I am sharing with you point out that the higher order
of Science is not just exclusive to Christian Science. It
is contained in any book which voices our divine oneness or which interprets our divinity. This is one reason
I have been introducing these books to you. You find
your identity and your harmony in them all.

Here is another letter I would like to share with you.
It is by a class-taught student who wrote this from her
high understanding.

In the higher order of Science students learn
that All is infinite Mind without any reserva-
tions whatever. They recognize every system
as a manifestation of Mind, indeed every ex-

---

89. Norman Cousins: *The Celebration of Life: A Dialogue On Immortality And Infinity.* Harper & Row, Publishers, New York, Copyright, 1974,
pages 68, 69, 82 and 83.

perience great or small. Too, they learn they
have a choice, and can translate any adverse
circumstance, seeing it Good, Mind manifest,
and they do not have to know how or why.
Holding to this sincerely and seeing clearly is
the Christ consciousness (cosmic consciousness) acting the moment total love takes over.
It cannot be forced, taught, or learned, but
it can be sought because it is *within every individual.* Walt Whitman writes: "I am the
mate and companion of people; all must be as
immortal and fathomless as myself. They do
not know how immortal, but *I* know."

I mentioned in *Identity* that the Bible is a source of
great substance. You can imagine my joy when I received another letter from the same person who wrote
the one above. In the second one she included several
statements from the Bible that she had beautifully translated into the higher order for herself. I cannot share
all of them but here are a few:

I will lift up mine eyes unto the hills, from
whence cometh my help.[90]

To this she writes: "I will see knowledge (unconfined
Spirit), Intelligence (Infinite Mind), Reason (Absolute
Truth), Understanding (universal divine love), Wisdom (law-enforcing Principle), Beauty (distinct individuality, Soul). These only can expand my thought and
life."

---

90. *Psalm* 121:1

My help *cometh* from the Lord, which made
heaven and earth.[91]

Her translation: "Expansion of my thought and life
comes from within me, from the centre of my being. It is
the gift of gifts; it is what I call the Vision that has
come ... My opportunity is to become better acquainted
with it and feel at ease in its presence; to comprehend
its power, availability and constant nearness. It requires
dedication, consecration, faith and utterable Love."

The Lord shall preserve thee from all evil: he
shall preserve thy soul.[92]

To this she says: "My vision stabilizes my being."

The Lord shall preserve thy going out and
thy coming in from this time forth, and even
for evermore.[93]

Her translation: "My vision monitors all the thoughts
coming into my consciousness and governs all the acts
I commit, all the conclusions I draw, all my thoughts."

In my classes on Identity, I included letters from those
who had received *The Bridge* and had commented
about it. Up to now I have not read you any of

91. *Psalm* 121:2
92. *Psalm* 121:7
93. *Psalm* 121:8

my answers to them. Many of these letters, however, contained particularly appropriate questions, and I feel it would be interesting to share what I wrote in reply to their questions on healing and organization using a composite letter. It may answer many of your own questions on these subjects. My letter is as follows:

> I arrived at the point of Allness knowing that there was *no one way* of healing. Since all healing is in the domain of the universal law of love, God, there can be no outlining as to the form or method of anyone's healing experience. *The Bridge,* as you know, brings this out in many ways. I am not puzzled anymore at the grand appearances of healing from many different sources; I just know that they are always glorious happenings and I rejoice and am glad.

> I suggest you read *Misc. Writs.,* pages 224: 11 through 27, beginning with ". . . the world is wide; that there are a thousand million different human wills, opinions, ambitions, tastes and loves . . ." This beautiful passage has always meant a great deal to me. Today I have a clearer view of the meaning of the word "culture." Healing in one culture is not the same as in another, but whatever the differences we cannot ignore the healings, when or where they occur, or from what source they come to comfort our mankind. They are forever presenting the Wholeness and Oneness of man.

In my own research (soul-searching) I have had to bow to love's infinity. I had to accept the seriousness of the healing work in orthodox Christian Science, its early stages of denial and affirmation, and I had to accept the Higher Order of Scientific Healing appearing as God-Realization, the Harmony of Being, the Science of Celestial Being.

My new premise includes gratitude for healings in Medical Science, Unity, in Religious Science, Divine Science, in the Pentacostal Movement, Transcendental Meditation, in Psychiatry, Psychology, Acupuncture, in Alcoholics Anonymous and in the work presently performed by the various evangelists of our day. These, in a sense, are all different cultures.

There are other avenues of healing also, and I do not mean to leave them out. The warm love of a mother for her child can work a miracle. The loving care of a friend, the influence of a book, of prayer beads, of an amulet, whatever — all are manifestations of the infinite Mind healing. I rejoice again in the glorious all-inclusiveness, forever unfolding, bringing peace, comfort and harmony to my mankind and my world. The moment you limit healing in any direction you limit the allness of God! Our premise claims God is infinite and on this basis avenues for healing are infinite also.

For the many paths of healing we have infinite gratitude; they are all directions of
love proving itself universally. We have had
limitations in our religious instruction where
it was outlined that healings must be obtained
through *one* source only—Christian Science.
With this we closed our minds to the infinity
of Love. In the higher order of healing the
doors open wide and we see divine love meeting *every* need, providing the God-consciousness that is the All-in-all.

I would like to share this with you from *The National
Observer,* June 26, 1976. It is a lengthy article about
Navajo Medicine Men: Healing Body and Soul, by
Suzanne Fields. Carl Gorman, a Navajo who is di-
rector of the Office of Native Healing Services, says
"Culture has a lot to do with healing. You must remember that the Anglo culture is very different from
the Navajo, and the Anglo approach will not always
work . . . The Anglo doctors used to laugh at us. But
many of them have come to realize that the Navajo
does not want to be treated for an injury only. His
mind also needs to be treated. He needs his medicine
man too."

In another letter I wrote the following in answer to
questions regarding organization:

The only reason that you have not been
able to free yourself from organizational and
ecclesiastical ties to The Mother Church
is that you still feel the church is your au-

thority. This is perfectly natural, of course, because you permitted it to be your authority for a great many years, and it is understandable that you are grateful for all the good that has been yours as a member, for your spiritual growth, for the activities your membership provided you, and for the unfoldment that has come to you through Christian Science instruction. These are some of the ties that bind you and, of course, you have friendships that you have made which may change if you modify your association with The Mother Church and the branch church.

There may be other ties also: relatives within the membership, for example. Sometimes we do not free ourselves because of pride. Since we have made it known that we are Christian Scientists it takes great courage to tell those who know us well that we have changed our religious commitment, or that we have had a renewal of inspiration and revelation. We may not appreciate criticism of this. Actually a new birth has occurred; we see things quite differently than before, but because of the influences I have described one is likely to stay in the organization rather than take a stand for the higher order of Science by openly admitting his advancing thoughts.

If this is your situation do not be unduly concerned because whether you realize it or not the Divine Mind, your mind, is reaching

for peace and a greater sense of harmony.
One's courage is always equal to his understanding, and as you find yourself happily
crossing your bridge, identifying with your
spiritual integrity, you come naturally into a
harmonious oneness and this is what the higher order of Science is all about.

You ask in your letter if we lose our friends
when we speak out and stand as Principle for
our higher ideals. Yes, we lose some of them,
but remember we lost friends when we became Christian Scientists. Divine love met
that human need, didn't it? The law of love
provides fulfillment for us at all times for
we are never absent from its encompassing
warmth. This same love takes care of our
friends, too, who feel they have lost us. Divine Love is meeting their need as well. This
is the law of love, the ever-presence that is
All-in-all.

Incidentally, Mrs. Eddy has much to say of such
experiences, although we pay very little attention to
what she says of them unless something in our life
turns us there. In referring to Jesus, she writes: ". . . his
brief triumphal entry into Jerusalem was followed by
the desertion of all save a few friends . . ."⁹⁴ and on
page 266 of *Science and Health* we read of some good
things about the *Uses of adversity,* but surely in the
higher order of Science we need never assume mar-

---

94. *S. & H.* 42:12-13

tyrdom at all. We rejoice in whatever occurs as well as how it occurs, realizing that our spiritual integrity has brought us where we are. We never cease to rejoice.

If you take a courageous stand for your highest understanding as Truth and if you state it to your teacher, to your practitioner or to your friends, you will always find the courage that is equal to your scientific understanding. The conviction of your honest intent gratifies the heart. Yes, all are blessed, all are companioned by the divine love which is. There is no loss that is not *immediately* seen as gain in this harmonious Christ-consciousness. Friendships are already prepared for us, ready and eager to share our new inspiration, ready to appreciate the light and harmony which springs from our new premise. There is no loss; only marvelous change, expansion and gain for all. Let us remember these encouraging words:

WAITING

I stay my haste, I make delays—
    For what avails this eager pace?
I stand amid eternal ways,
    And what is mine shall know my face.

Asleep, awake, by night or day,
    The friends I seek are seeking me.
No wind can drive my bark astray
    Nor change the tide of destiny.

* * *

The waters know their own, and draw
  The brooks that spring in yonder heights;
So flows the good with equal law
  Unto the soul of pure delight.

The stars come nightly to the sky;
  The tidal wave unto the sea;
Nor time, nor space, nor deep, nor high
  Can keep my own away from me.[95]

As for my feelings regarding organization I might
well quote a timely statement: ". . . strait *is* the gate,
and narrow *is* the way, which leadeth unto life, and
few there be that find it."[96] I often thought my membership in the Christian Science Church was this narrow way leading me into the ". . . Life divine, that
owns each waiting hour . . ,"[97] and perhaps this was
true because my wishes to go beyond the dualistic interpretations have led me into a universal Allness, into
a wider meaning of Truth, of healing, of life and love.
I could not remain with the narrowness of orthodoxy,
but I found within its instruction the way to a broader
view, and I had no hesitancy in following it into the
Higher Order of Science that Mrs. Eddy speaks about
in *Miscellaneous Writings*. Now I should like to return
to my composite letter:

You write here of the memory of the Association meetings you attended and you re-

---

95. John Burroughs: *Waiting*. THE LIGHT OF DAY. Houghton Mifflin Co., Boston, Mass. 02107.
96. *Matthew* 7:4
97. *Christian Science Hymnal* #207

call the marvelous advancement you experienced. Well, this is true, but infinite Mind does not stop advancing; it simply brings you into higher views and wider fields, into a more satisfying fulfillment. In *The Bridge* I stated on page 283 how I settled things for myself: ". . . I realized from this interview [with a prominent Christian Science practitioner] that I would not seek corroboration of the Oneness concept anymore from practitioners, teachers, or lecturers within the organization [because I knew I would no longer find it there]." Incidentally, in line with this I feel that one of the most important parts of *The Bridge* is in the chapter on *Man, Present Being,* beginning on page 274 with the words: "To conclude this chapter . . ." and ending on page 283 with ". . . daily teaching the Oneness."

You say here that it is your gratitude that keeps you bound. Well, Jesus was bound in gratitude to the Judaic Laws, yet he found himself voicing a higher order of Love *within* the Judaic structure. He found, too, that he had to separate himself from a straight and narrow way to explore his own divinity, and in his exploration he went beyond his Judaic religious background to bring us what we know today as Christianity. This does not mean that we throw Judaism away. Surely we appreciate much of what we find in the Old Testament, and the Lesson-Sermons in Christion Science certainly pay a great deal of attention to it, but we have had no hesitation in accepting the New Testament because these books conform to our own advancement. Jesus gave us a more enlightened understanding of Life, Truth and Love and a personal interpretation of God as Father, not as an impersonal Supreme Being to fear but, rather, one to love.

In the higher order of Science I am introducing a very personal God which is within you and not at all something outside or apart from your divine nature. Jesus was grateful for the good reports of the Old Testament, but he could not endorse all of it so he translated much of it for himself by finding his own identity in it. Of course his personal inspiration is available to benefit us if we choose. I feel that this is precisely what I have done with Mrs. Eddy's works. After studying them conscientiously, I concluded that I could not agree with many of her ideas any longer, but I held fast to those with which I could identify and those that were bringing out total Oneness, called by some the absolute or Divine Science.

How can you be outside of God's Allness? You know by the very definition that this is impossible. Not even those who have never heard of Christianity or Christian Science are outside of Love's Allness. Love cares, is inter-

ested, is concerned, governs and directs everyone regardless of race, color or creed. The harmony of your Being results from your assurance that Love (God) just IS, now and forever. Of course you should not be afraid.
"Perfect love casteth out fear." You should
read again the chapter in *The Bridge* on *The
Translation of Animal Magnetism,* and accept the glorious understanding that God is
ALL—not only sometime but *all the time.*

Work out your harmony of being as others
have done by reaching daily for your highest concept of good. Then accept your best
conviction and apply it practically, personally
and spiritually to your immediate life. Don't
just talk about it; give it visible expression in
good deeds. You see, as long as you are re-
taining the fears you are expressing in your
letter you are not fully convinced of your own
divinity, are you? You ask, "Am I still believ-
ing in a power opposed to God which will
judge or condemn me?" Well, you remember
how Jesus, though condemned by the multi-
tude, walked through the crowd untouched.
This is your experience, too, for Love is your
strengthening power.

In the Higher Order of Love we understand what criticism by another really is: it
represents that person's highest understanding of a situation, maybe not ours, but it is
his nevertheless. We do not think ill of him

because of his judgments of us; we love him, and this sets us free. Our harmony and peace remain with us, and we walk on, learning what we need to—even changing if necessary —and we rejoice in our developing understanding, seeing Love always triumphant.

———————

Now, having finished with my composite letter, may I go on to relate a story about "body"—the human form, the physical evidence of Spirit.

A woman, discussing her problems with me one day, said that she needed to get into her closet more, meaning her place of prayer, so she could be absent from her body to be present with the Lord. She told me this in such an earnest way that it sounded as though she was about to have a very religious experience. I knew what she meant: she wanted to get her personal, material, human concept out of the way so she could relate to a spiritual power outside of herself! She was surprised when I told her that trying to do this was actually a return to the old work of annihilation. She wanted to deny her existence, her very own life, her visible identity. I told her I used to work this way when I was receiving the instruction of Christian Science and I even mentioned some of the details I have written in *The Bridge* about metaphysical work I had done. But now my view is different. I do not try to get physicality out of the way because I see it as my divinity. I agree with John M. Dorsey who said, "Mind is the body of which Self-awareness is the Soul." We do not have to shut ourselves out to let God in. *God is the In Experience in the higher order of Science.*

Regarding the thought of body there is an interesting story which is told about Mrs. Eddy. It explained a great deal to me during my advance into the higher order. One day while having lunch with some of her students she was asked what would happen to her body if someone came in and shot her and the shot was fatal. She is reported to have said, "You would think I was dead, but I would go right on eating my apple." Accepting the validity of her statement I would feel that she was pointing out to her students her own advancement into a higher order of Body, higher than the statements she gave them in the instruction where they are repeatedly told to deny the physical senses because they are erroneous. Assuming the story to be true, she was seeing a body that she believed to be indestructible and eternal, and the body that she saw as Mrs. Eddy was her fleshly body. This is what she was talking about and this is what was eating the apple. She was saying that that particular body would not be destroyed; it would simply go right on being her body even though she might appear to be dead. In this she was explaining the eternality of her Being.

My own metaphysical work in the instruction of Christian Science became one which deleted as many of the negative statements on "body" as possible, replacing them with more substantial definitions. Paul Brunton says: "Know yourself without losing your awareness . . . Self *is* Being—consciousness." Oddly enough it was my own dedication as a practitioner which led me to a higher concept of body. In my work I often looked in the concordances for references on *body.* Up to a certain time I was satisfied with what I found. Later I was not. Why? Because I found that the instruction kept me working dualistically, and this became no longer satisfying to me. The divinity course within my reasoning self advanced me to a more absolute approach. "Spirit is positive." (*Science and Health,* page 173, line 13). When I accepted the truth of this, I knew at last that it was the *spirit within me* demanding new criteria in my work.

You may recall how enthusiastic I was in my introduction of Jan Christiaan Smuts in *The Bridge.* I stated he was a biologist, and that, in describing his world of matter, life and mind, he coined a word, naming it "holism." It represented to him a wholeness of nature unified in a divine and systematic Oneness and Allness. His universe of people, places and things resolved itself into a harmonious whole. This integration, this synthesis, is the harmonizing of one's self to one's universe and this is what we have discovered in the higher order of Science.

Now I am just as joyous in introducing to you a book entitled *Illness or Allness* written by the same John M. Dorsey I previously quoted. You will find the theme of Oneness brought out many times in its pages. I would like to share a great deal of it with you, but now may I share these two excerpts?

> My true birth dated from the day I, for the first time, saw consciously my identity in my every experience. I knew then what Shakespeare meant by his words, "Before, I loved thee as a brother, John. But now I do respect thee as my soul." I said to myself, *"There* is

god, and he is myself." No longer did it suf-
fice for me to say that "god is great," and
thus conceal my very own divine magnitude.
Without this divine self-love I can conceive
of neither sight nor insight for myself. It was
only by my discovering my divinity that I was
able to discover the divinity in everyone of my
world.[98]

Love underlies and supports the grateful ap-
preciation of wholeness of individuality. Love
unifies, harmonizes, synthesizes, and thus up-
holds the truth of oneness. Love is the principle of pure pleasure which enables the learner
to see that his life is worth living and that
each of his life lessons is worth learning.[99]

These are truly great thoughts. To me they represent a very high order of Self, and written by a psychiatrist, no less! This book is worth serious study by
everyone; it is just another proof that fundamental
statements of pure Science are not only to be found in
Science and Health, written one hundred years ago.
They are also in the minds of men discovered and infinitely expressed today as well as yesterday.

———————

I want to preface this next story with a statement
we all know: "Divine Love always has met and always

98. John M. Dorsey, M.D.: *Illness or Allness.* Wayne State University
Press, Detroit. Copyright, 1965, page 480.
99. *Ibid.,* p. 151.

will meet every human need."[100] When we do not outline how this divine love is to appear we are sometimes
astonished at how infinitely it provides for all of us.

A friend of ours made a trip west. He was to be
interviewed for a position in Los Angeles because he
had decided to leave his work in the east and seek em-
ployment elsewhere. He told me that his family situation was not what he felt it should be. He and his wife
had separated. They have several children and he was
very concerned about it all. He was very frank in telling me that since his wife became interested in Christian Science she wanted him to appreciate its teachings but it was not easy for him to accept the doctrine.
Although he tried he could not understand the instruction, and he felt he should not be going to church if
it did not mean something to him spiritually.

They had been to a marriage counselor, but this had
not helped. As there was a very obvious disinclination
to talk about Christian Science even from my premise,
I found myself asking him if he ever read a book entitled, *I'M OK—YOU'RE OK*. He had not. I told
him that it might interest him, that there was a chapter in it on marriage which might shed some light on
his situation. When he left he took it with him, and
later I had an opportunity to talk with him on the telephone. He told me that he had found it *most* helpful, that he had given it to his wife and his oldest
daughter to read. Within a short time he was back
with his family, had found a new job, and had moved
into a beautiful new home. From the recent letters I

---

100. *S. & H.* 494:10-11

have received they are very happy; they have a new harmony of being and they are blessed by it.

When he returned the book he explained his liking for it by saying that it gave him a working premise with which to guide his affairs. So we learn again that "Love is impartial and universal in its adaptation and bestowals."[101] The desire for harmony brought the necessary solution to this man and his family at least to some degree through the book he borrowed. Love's impartiality finds solutions in diverse places, sometimes in those we would least suspect, but love is there all the time.

Yes, "every one that thirsteth, come ye to the waters," and do not outline where these waters should come from. Love does not wonder at its source; it knows only of its infinity and its availability. As we live more of this harmony of being we meet the needs of others more universally and are led quite naturally to supply them in ways that make this love more easily understood and, therefore, more readily received.

How wonderful for each of us to get beyond the limiting concept that *our* way is the only way! The first words in the preface to *Science and Health* are: "To those leaning on the *sustaining infinite,* to-day is big with blessings" (italics mine). How these blessings appear are individual and unique, but we must have faith in our own infinite sustenance. Just a simple and sincere desire (prayer, acknowledgement) for harmony may be sufficient to start a whole new life. Many opportunities come to us to open wide the doors for love to take care of that desire. Whatever, the *pray-er and*

---

101. *S. & H.* 13:2-3

the prayer are One. Any self-righteousness proclaiming only *one* path, *one* road or *one* way shrinks before the person who knows the tremendous power of universal love.

After recommending *I'M OK—YOU'RE OK* to a Christian Scientist she wrote: "Yes, it is good. I saw many things reminding me of *The Bridge*. The first paragraph on page four, for instance,—how identical to *The Bridge*'s thrust forward, and he brings out one's freedom to choose, a point which *The Bridge* emphasizes again and again." This is what she is referring to:

> What I hope to demonstrate in this book is a new way to state old ideas and a clear way to present new ones, not as an inimical or deprecating assault on the work of the past, but rather as a means of meeting the undeniable evidence that the old methods do not seem to be working very well.[102]

Let us continue with two more references from this book:

> We cannot guarantee instant OK feelings by the assuming of the *I'M OK—YOU'RE OK* position. We have to be sensitive to the presence of the old recordings; but we can choose to turn them off when they replay in a way that undermines the faith we have in a new

---

102. Thomas A. Harris, M.D., *I'M OK—YOU'RE OK,* Harper and Row, Publishers, New York, page 4, copyright 1963.

way to live, which, *in time,* will bring forth
new results and new happiness in our living.[103]

In *I'M OK—YOU'RE OK* the question is asked:
"How Does a Religious Experience Feel?" and the author's reply on page 237 is:

> Persons report religious experience to be more
> like a Presence of God rather than knowledge
> about God. It perhaps is truly ineffable, and
> its only objective validation may be the
> change it may effect in a person's life. This
> change is seen in people who are able to re-
> move the NOT OK from positions they have
> held about themselves and others. Deciding
> on the position I'M OK—YOU'RE OK has
> been reported as a conversion experience.

———

In our work in orthodoxy we either oversimplified
or we became too complicated and too labored. Somewhere along the way the consecrated student finds himself reaching out to a spiritual experience that is as
natural as it is marvelously simple. The simplicity of it
points to the divine Oneness already within him as a
living reality. Fresh and beautiful essences exist as form
and color, majestic attributes singularly defined, each
object of creation magnificently unique and glorious,
and of these *we deny nothing.* All of them reach into

———

103. Thomas A. Harris, M.D.: *I'M OK—YOU'RE OK.* Harper and Row,
Publishers, New York, page 53, copyright, 1963.

our view, and we appreciate, praise and rejoice in the
harmony of our present beautiful universe.

At a time when our home in Connecticut (Treasure
Hill) was in its early spring bloom, I invited my teacher and his wife to visit us. Our dogwood trees (all 15
of them), some white and others pink, were in full
flower. In my enthusiasm I pointed them out to him.
His understanding of the Truth (as he so correctly
stated it from the orthodox view) informed me there
was no multiplicity in Mind, and therefore in substance
and in truth, as well as in form and color, there was
but *ONE* dogwood and that it existed in Mind, but
only as a spiritual idea. As such it could not possibly
appear objectively as the many dogwoods I was seeing. In the way I accepted my Science at that time I
was more than willing to be corrected. I was receptive
to the spiritual, invisible idea of dogwood, so I let my
fifteen, beautiful, material manifestations of lovely dogwoods go! I could not dispute his correction, for in the
instruction we are told that the realm of the real is
Spirit, and that what we see with our material, mortal
eyes is not the real beauty. It is a misconception and
should be relegated to its "native nothingness."

Within me after this, however, doubts of many kinds
arose, and sometime later I visited my teacher in his
office in New York to discuss some things with him.
One of the questions I asked him was this: If one had
no idea what a dogwood looked like materially how
could he have a spiritual idea of it? Good question! My
teacher did not answer it; instead he held fast to the
misconception of material things feeling that by so doing no answer would be needed. He repeated that these
ideas flourish as Spirit but are forever invisible to us

in our mortality. I was not convinced, not with my growing awareness of reality, here, now. However I went on sincerely desiring a fulfillment of present reality, and I found it as I willingly accepted a higher order of my universe. My dogwoods *were* representations of many variations of ideas, materially, in all their beauteous adornment, living, dying, and being forever reborn—a state of foreverness. I lived at Treasure Hill long enough to see them in every form and stage of life, their life divine, and I appreciated their snow-covered season of no blossoms as well as their full blossoming in springtime and throughout the summers.

As I accepted the Science of Celestial Being, a wonderful sense of spiritual satisfaction came to me. In it I have found myself tuned to broader interpretations of kinship with *all* life, and I have developed a growing awareness of the reverence we must have for this kinship in all its areas in order to be the pure Science. I have found this in many ways. The marginal heading for the first part of the following statement is *"Self-completeness."* "As mortals gain *more correct views* of God and man, multitudinous objects of creation, which before were invisible, *will become visible."*[104] All we have to do is to let these correct views be entertained; let "correct views" be what our minds accept. Nothing ever needs to be given up or destroyed.

Restoration of the truth about the material universe is our metaphysical approach in the higher order of Science, *not its denial.* We behold the spiritual/material beauty and continue to wonder at its infinite manifestation. With this understanding not only are

---

104. *S. & H.* 264:13-15 (Italics mine).

our dogwoods restored to us but so much more! For this reason I cannot today agree with Mrs. Eddy's statement on page 267, lines 1 and 2 of *Science and Health* that "Every object in material thought will be destroyed, but the spiritual idea, whose substance is in Mind, is eternal." This Mind and its eternality is the substance which I am now, spirit indestructible. Even at this moment of writing I remember last fall watching leaves falling from our birch tree, but now in the spring I see glorious newness appearing in the fullness of its being.

This idea of restoration is found in the Bible. It is the story of the disciples, still bound by the scribe's authority. They came to remind Jesus that ". . . Elias must first come." To this Jesus answered, ". . . Elias truly shall first come, and *restore* all things," and then unhesitatingly he translated this *as himself* for he quickly stated ". . . Elias *is come already* . . ."[105] meaning that his personal presence as the Messiah, the Christ, Jesus, the person, represented Elias' coming. Now raise this to your own Being; *restore all things* harmoniously by realizing that Elias has come to you as *your divine Self*.

We read ". . . the sweet harmonies of Christian Science are found to correct the discords of sense, and to lift man's being into the sunlight of Soul."[106] Our work in the traditional instruction of Christian Science was to correct the discords of sense based on the assumption that sense was discordant and that it had to be seen as error, a misconception, in order to be corrected.

---

105. *Matthew* 17:10, 11, 12 (Italics mine).
106. *Mis.* 202:2-4

Many Lesson-Sermons directed us how to do this. In the higher order of Science, however, not only do we see sense as *concordant* but *we lift our being into the sunlight of Soul* and keep it there, sustained by our understanding of Celestial Reality. We emphasize statements that remind us of the pure essence of our Science, one of which is "Mind, joyous in strength, dwells in the realm of Mind. Mind's infinite ideas run and disport themselves. In humility they climb the heights of holiness."[107] Let us ". . . Be allied to the deific power, and [know that] all that is good will aid . . . [our] journey . . ."[108] These statements recognize the Science of your harmonious Being.

This may be as good a time as any other to bring out an important part of my work. There have been sincere friends who felt that I quoted Mrs. Eddy more than I should have because I repeatedly revealed how much I had outgrown the early instruction of Christian Science. The latter is true, but of all the books that I have read, and all the sermons I have had occasion to listen to, and all the inspirational messages I have heard on radio and on television, I feel that what Mrs. Eddy said *in her exalted writings* bespeaks the ultimate for a positive approach to life and love. But one must exclude her dualism and translate all to the advancing thoughts that are there. The message I give in my

107. *S. & H.* 514:6-9
108. *Un.* 17:5-6

classes is to promote the higher order found within her
works, for this is her greatness.

When John Steinbeck tried to explain to his dear
friend and publisher, Pascal Covici, about the ending
of the famous *Grapes of Wrath,* this is what he gave
him to think about:

> Throughout I've tried to make the reader
> participate in the actuality; what he takes
> from it will be scaled entirely on his own
> depth or hollowness. There are five layers in
> this book; a reader will find as many as he
> can and he won't find more than he has in
> himself.[109]

In my own study of Mary Baker Eddy's writings, I
do believe that I consistently went through all the layers
in them, and when my own Divinity Course led me to
her highest concepts I knew that I had found something very precious indeed. I shared it as best I could
in my practice until I felt the need to share it with
other Christian Scientists through my books. Some
friends and relatives have felt that what I have written
should not have been limited to the field of Christian
Science and that I would have reached a greater audience if I had not used the initials C.S. But Christian
Science has been the direction my life has taken and
its purpose I know now has been to interpret the higher
order of Christian Science, which I feel is the most
important layer found within its teachings. Why? Be-

---

109. *Steinbeck: A Life In Letters.* Edited by Elaine Steinbeck and Robert
Wallsten, The Viking Press, Inc. Copyright 1975, pp 178-179.

cause in it the individual resolves the dualistic dilemma, finally identifying with an absolute Oneness wherein he attains a lasting harmony and is ready to live his vision infinite.

———

Let me refer you to some grand and noble references to make your own. "Man in the likeness of God as revealed in Science cannot help being immortal."[110] This man has certainly been revealed to you in your work. It is yourself, and all you have to do is to identify with Godliness and be in harmony with your mortal-immortal being. Then consider this statement: "To live so as to keep human consciousness in constant relation with the divine, the spiritual, and the eternal, is to individualize infinite power; and this is Christian Science."[111] We are directed to keep our human natures in *constant relation* with the divine and by so doing we individualize the power of infinite love in our daily lives. With the personal, *human you* in this relationship with the *divine you,* the mortality and the immortality of you are in union *as* you. Think about this. It means that your eternality is established at the very moment that you take this statement to your heart! Do not leave it in a book, to be read for the next hundred years! Letting it *be you* should make the following quotation acceptable to you:

"Man is a celestial; and in the spiritual universe he is forever individual and forever harmonious."[112] This

110. *S. & H.* 81:17-18
111. *My.* 160:5-8
112. *No.* 26:24-25

is the grand layer for you to accept. Surely you recognize these last few quotations as the higher order of
your Self. This is the Science that is meaningful to us
today which we love to impart. It is your Christ, your
harmony, your divine nature as it has always been and
is forever. Your soul sense identifies as this harmony.
We do not seek to live *above* corporeality; we take our
humanness into our spiritual reality where they both
exist in holy habitation; we live it here in full awareness of the spiritual *reality* of body, the mansion of our
divinity. A friend of mine, Leah Bohn, C.S., expressed
her spiritual habitation this way in a poem which she
sent in a letter to me:

MY SECRET HOUSE

I, too, have a secret house!
It is remembering—
Remembering what I am!
I am the silent splendor of the dawn

That blooms as day.
I am the stillness of the forest
And the warm shafted sunlight
On the squirrels at play.

I am the lullaby
Of the wind in the trees,
And the song of the birds
On the wings of the breeze.

I am the sound of summer rain
On the roof . . . or sometimes
The dancing moonbeams
On my lake, or the coral bell's chimes.

Whatever I do,
Wherever I go . . .
I've a house of my own
That only I know.

If I am lonely or ever afraid
Of wanting to touch a star,
My heart says remember—always remember
What you are!

"The physical Reality, man, and the spiritual Reality, man, are one and the same thing when we have done our work properly on the higher plane of Christian Science. Let us not work *toward* Oneness, but let us accept it for ourselves, now, ourselves in spirit/flesh and soul/body unity."[113]

Divine Science directs us to live a more divine us. We have happily accepted the Reality of Being not because we have given up mortal, human, material concepts, *but because we have raised them to the understanding that they are the very substance of all that is spiritual and eternal, our personal divinity!* We do not leave the old for the new; we simply take the inspiration of the past and translate it to our present. Then mortality, our human, material selfhood, is with

---

113. Irene S. Moore, C.S.: *The Bridge.* DeVorss and Co., Publishers, Marina del Rey, California, page 236. Copyright, 1971.

us more gloriously, presenting our divinity in a way that we may not have seen or felt before because now we are putting into action the premise that life is eternal and harmonious forever.

Isn't this wonderful: "Deity was satisfied with His work"?[114] This must be our very own satisfaction as well; what a joyous thing it is to be satisfied! Rejoice in it! And isn't this a good thing to know: "From Love [which you are] and from the light and harmony . . . [which you are as] the abode of Spirit . . ."[115] only expressions of Good (not reflections) can come? I have introduced some phrases into this statement, the marginal heading for which is *The things of God are beautiful,* the very things that are presently ours. They comprise our spiritual habitation and, even though you already know it, I joyously add it is here in the flesh that we dwell in holiness and harmony.

A very dear friend of mine was disturbed when she heard I had written a book which incorporated many of the ideas of Oneness we had often discussed and which she professed to understand and accept. She felt, however, the publication of this book might stir the field too much and that this in turn, through her friendship with me, might adversely influence her position with the members of her church as well as with our mutual friends. For many years she had enjoyed

114. *S. & H.* 519:3
115. *S. & H.* 280:4-5

my inspiration but when my higher order of Science was finally in book form she rejected it.

Soon after *The Bridge* was published, she informed me quite honestly that although she appreciated my advancing thoughts she would be unable to read the book, not because it was unauthorized, for she had read many books of this nature, but because she did not want to be in a position of having to discuss it with her friends. She said that if she did not read it she would be freed of having to answer any questions about it. Her frankness was sincere and I simply had to realize the time for her to acknowledge an understanding of the higher order of Science publicly had not yet arrived, even though I knew she had begun to put more emphasis on the Oneness concept in her metaphysical work as a Christian Scientist while she was coming out of the dualism of orthodoxy. She told me she was more secure remaining within the organization with her many Christian Science friends at this time of her life. I had a great compassion for her and taking her in my arms I let her know that I understood her feelings completely.

One of the themes running throughout *The Bridge* and *Identity* is that every individual is operating at his highest understanding; he is *Person, Man, Present Being* and there is, therefore, no place for criticism, for dismay or disappointment in anyone. Total love takes command. I am sharing this story with you to make it very clear that whatever direction our relationship with others may take, our harmony remains intact within us, unchanged even when another's point of view casts doubt upon our actions. We see where he is, and we bless him and understand why.

We let each person remain in his spiritual habitation, the one he has established for himself, and we see it as Good. Jesus understood Peter's denial of him, but he also knew that that very denial would eventually become the rock, the strength, the affirmation of the Christ Truth which Peter was and knew and loved.

Harmonious being in interpersonal relationships demands that we let each one work out his salvation where he is. We know divine love is the center and circumference of *his* being just as it is for ourselves and for all others with whom we come in contact, for that matter even those we do not know. This makes us all substantially One; none is outside of Love's provision. Love's many directives surround us, establishing our God-Being as we understand it today and identifying us as this higher order of Love.

We learn to express ourselves as "The great I AM; the all-knowing, all-seeing, all-acting, all-wise, all-loving and eternal . . ."[116] The presence of these qualities as *us* and the acknowledgment of our God-Being, governs and directs us to say the loving thing and to do the loving thing, that is: to *be* love. Each of us is living his life religiously, divinely, scientifically, wisely, philosophically, and lovingly as he chooses to live it, and since all is mind and its infinite expression, each one is living his divinity *at every stage of unfoldment*. I suggest you read again pages 64 and 65 of *The Bridge* regarding the *Scientific Translation Of Immortal Mind* and the *Scientific Translation Of Mortal Mind, First Degree*: Depravity, *Second Degree*: Evil beliefs disappearing, *Third Degree*: Understanding. Now take

---

116. *S. & H.* 587:5-6

the definition of Judah in the *Glossary,* page 589, and
see how well you answer this question for yourself in
the Higher Order of Science: Are you, "A corporeal
material belief progressing and disappearing . . ." or
are you ". . . the spiritual understanding of God and
man appearing"?

Although there is only one reference in Mrs. Eddy's
writings to Gad, Jacob's son who later became King
David's seer, I would like to spend a few minutes on
the definition given us in the *Glossary*: "Gad (Jacob's
son). Science; spiritual being understood; haste towards harmony."[117]

The history of this man as a spiritual being interested
me, particularly his ". . . haste [desire] towards harmony." Born of Leah's maid Zilpah and rising through
his spiritual heritage to become King David's seer and
warrior, we learn that he overcame many difficult
situations. Not only did he surmount his problems but
when he came to the land of Gilead for a possession,
Moses identified him with this beautiful thought:
"Blessed be he that enlargeth Gad . . ."[118] We might
translate this as "Blessed be Gad in desiring within his
being to understand the Harmony of his scientific Self."
Gad's experience was one of valor, strength, courage
and obedience coupled with an awareness of his spiritual heritage.

In Revelation, 4 through 7, we understand that Gad
was among those who had reached the harmony of his
being, and remained secure in the spiritual habitation
of his peace and joy. We here today have our own

---

117. *S. & H.* 586:21-22
118. *Deuteronomy* 33:20

spiritual habitation and we may rejoice that through the higher order of Science the acceptance of our spiritual being is now fully understood.

You may recall an article in *The Christian Science Monitor,* November 20th, 1974, by Frederick Hunt, entitled *Religious Ferment in America: Appeal of Eastern Religions.* It is all worth reading, but the part I wish to share is a statement by Richard Harrington, a former University of Toronto philosophy instructor who now belongs to a Christian commune in California. He says: "Everything deeply understood leads to God . . ." and by "everything" he means all religions and creeds and philosophic concerns with life, death and creation. I feel that when the Eastern religions are sufficiently understood by us, God, Good, will be seen in them as All just as in religions we know better.

This leads me to make some comment about the Maharishi Yogi. Not long ago a class-taught Christian Scientist with many years of membership in the organization told me she had become interested in the *Transcendental Meditation* technique. In our conversations she was happy to learn that I was well aware of it. I had read several books on the subject and, having seen the Maharishi on television, I was impressed with the calm joy and with the loving, universal thoughts he expressed. Moreover, other guests on the program lent support to everything he said about the technique, many of them telling the audience how it had helped in organizing and directing their lives with satisfying results. May I say now: anyone who hesitates to read about eastern philosophies and religions should realize that the roots of our Bible spring from many of these ideas and that Jesus was masterfully familiar with them, expressing the same or similar thoughts within the context of his own culture. Christianity contains more similarities with eastern concepts than differences.

Since my own emergence into a higher order of understanding I find myself interested in anyone who cares to share his unfoldment of peace, joy and inspiration with me. In reading *The Science Of Being And Art Of Living* by Maharishi Yogi I realized that any student of Christian Science who has crossed his bridge by identifying with his Science of Celestial Being can find many ideas in this philosophy with which he can joyously agree if he will let go of the taboos about orientalism. Many Christian Scientists today explore these religious values from the East without feeling guilty for having done it. There was, in fact, a student in this class who shared with us a meeting she had attended on the *Transcendental Meditation* technique, and we enjoyed what she gave us. Although I have stressed the religious content of the Maharishi's chapter on The Fulfilment of Religion, I understand this to be only a small part of the holistic concept of his book. There are four major parts to this volume: The Science Of Being, Life, The Art Of Living, and Fulfilment.

Let me offer you some of the statements from the Maharishi's book:

Religion is a way, or at least should be a way, to raise the consciousness of man to the level of God-consciousness and the human mind to the level of divine intelligence or universal cosmic mind.[119]

The true spirit of religion is lacking if it merely lays down what is right or wrong and creates the fear of punishment and hell and the fear of God in the minds of men. The purpose of religion should be to take away all fear.[119]

Next to the above statement I wrote in the margin of this book, "Yes. That is why I was inspired to write a chapter in *The Bridge* entitled, *The Translation of Animal Magnetism*."

Religion should be strong enough to bring to the individual in a natural manner a state of fulfilment in life without strenuous practices or long years of training. If it is fully integrated in itself, a religion should enable man to live fulfilment naturally.[119]

A fully alive and integrated religion will be one through which each man becomes a man of realized God-consciousness, a man enjoying the full values of life, a man of God; the Divine manifested in the form of man on earth.[119]

---

119. Maharishi Mahesh Yogi: *The Science Of Being And Art Of Living*. International SRM Publication, 1966, pp 255, 257.

This book supports the universal love found as the higher order of Science within Christian Science. I suggest that you read it and identify with its high purpose for you. On page 258 in the chapter on *The Fulfilment Of Religion,* I found this:

> Life should be such that religion is lived naturally with its purpose fulfiled. It should not be a struggle to live or attain fulfilment. Life should be lived in fulfilment of all its values. Man on earth, a man of real, lively and integrated religion, should be a living god, the Divine speaking, not a struggling man with faith in God searching for the meaning of the Divine. The substance of God, the status of God, the existence of God, God consciousness, divine consciousness—all these should be the natural life of man.

In the margin next to the above quotation I have written the word *IDENTITY.*

These last quotations have been true in my own experience in Christian Science. As I reached out beyond the instruction, I found the *higher meanings* waiting as my own harmonious, divine unfoldment, and I must repeat I found them *within Christian Science* when I was willing to give up the premise of dualism. While this premise is set up for the beginner in Christian Science, the natural sequel to it as one moves ahead is the premise of Oneness which is also there, and it is on this basis that the advancing student finds his understanding. Again I quote, this time from page 260 of the Maharishi's book:

A religious life should be one lived in bliss,
joyfulness, peace, harmony, creativity and intelligence.

My inevitably recurring delight has been to find
more and more of these universal truths arriving from
a great many sources. I am very much like what is
meant by the little cartoon someone sent me in the
mail. It showed only a pair of eyes! Below it, this
caption: "It's strange, but wherever I take my eyes,
they always see things from my point of view."

Much in this book by Maharishi Yogi came to me
after I had had my own divinity course in Christian
Science, and after I had written two books. Of course
truths he has written have been stated before but their
arrangement makes his ideas convincing, and they are
sincere, inspired and true. Mrs. Eddy in her higher
order of thinking has said the same things in a different language and another style, a Victorian one,
perhaps one more poetic. I am grateful for them both.
Today I am appreciating more than ever the fulfillment of the Harmony of my Being because I know
love to be its universal foundation. It is a venturesome
experience to find identification in so many places. I
see truth in them because I found it first *within* myself.
Finding it here I see it everywhere.

In the definition for *God* in the *Glossary*, we find
that the last word is *intelligence* and if you look in your
concordances you will find that the relationship made
again and again is that *God is intelligence*. This denotes

a great spiritual fact about ourselves: "Controlled by the divine intelligence, man is harmonious and eternal."[120] Now with our work with identity we know that the God within us is this divine intelligence, and this withinness which abounds in all areas of our lives constitutes our harmony. Then it follows that as God is intelligence so are you intelligence. A further spiritual elevation for you is knowing "INTELLIGENCE. Substance; self-existent and eternal Mind; that which is never unconscious nor limited"[121] to be the fundamental nature of your divinity here and now.

Following this reference we turn to page 469 of *Science and Health* where we find the answer to the question: "What is intelligence?" I ask you to identify with its definition: "Intelligence is omniscience, omnipresence, and omnipotence. It is the primal and eternal quality of infinite Mind, of the triune Principle,— Life, Truth, and Love,—named God." Since you have already identified with the synonyms for God and have acknowledged your Oneness, you should find it naturally and divinely satisfying to know this *intelligence* to be *you*. Now go a step further with the definition of *Creator* in the *Glossary,* reading lines 20-22 *only,* because if you continue further you are introduced to something extraneous to *Creator* which you will have to *unsee*—the kind of work you had to do in the elementary instruction of Christian Science.

In the Harmony of our Being we do not have battles between opposites; we remain consistent with our present divinity and its premise of Oneness. Mrs. Eddy says

---

120. *S. & H.* 184:16-17
121. *S. & H.* 588:24-25

human thoughts must turn to the divine Mind as their center and intelligence, and that until this is done man will never be harmonious. She is saying that the center and intelligence of *human* thought can be the divine mind. So, let it be! How important it is for us to accept this as our divine makeup! In recognizing its greatness we cannot possibly annihilate personality or individuality; instead of this we elevate them to their divine level where they manifest their real identity. There is great freedom in not having to compare "evil forces" of material intelligence with spiritual intelligence of God, Good. Your higher order of Science gives you that freedom, and with it the harmony that follows. When one stays within his spiritual habitation he finds the material-versus-spiritual belief dissolving and in its place is the divine expression unadulterated, pure and true.

I remember writing to my teacher about attending a Bible course being held in Los Angeles. His letter to me suggested I would get more from my continued work in Christian Science and that these added studies might introduce human beliefs and material conjecture which would distract me from the spiritual foundation I already had. Following his advice at that time I did not take the course, but later someone gave me the book on which it had been based, and in reading it I was wonderfully inspired by its concentrated study of the Apocalypse. It did not distract me in any way; in fact it gave me a fresh point of view, one which actually enhanced my understanding of Christian Science! The truth within me recognized that my God-intelligence was part of the all-knowing function of my very own divine mind. Since then I have been humbly grateful for the different interpretations that are meeting the human need, comforting, guiding, explaining, inspiring and identifying.

It is easy to see that each individual gravitates toward the religious explanation which harmonizes with his spiritual nature. In the higher order of intelligent Being we enjoy investigating all manner of religious concepts. We appreciate whatever the form because we know all are parts of our expanding material/spiritual universe with its divine and harmonious happenings. In *The Bridge,* on page 63, I wrote, "There is no denying other religions their divine part in the reality of Being nor is there any denying of one's right to other forms of healing. Mind is there where man is and surely Love loves enough to operate infinitely. We see that wherever the interest or therapy is going on, whatever its growth, insight, or revelation, on every level Mind is operating for our mankind, our universe, in every occurence. In the understanding that all there is to my universe and to man is divine tolerance and Love I do not "miss-see" anything; I *see* the the law of harmony right here."

Incidentally one of Webster's definitions of *an* intelligence is "An intelligent being or spirit: specifically an angel." I like this because it defines our capabilities. We can be angels anywhere, any place and any time, and I am talking about an "angel" as a celestial being, a personal messenger of truth and love here on earth. Being one is not outside of us; it happens to be our spiritual habitation. At Christmas time I made doll houses for my neighbor's children. On each little table in the doll's living room I had placed a little angel, and after the children had received them and had been playing with them for a while, one of them asked me if I could take the wings off the angel. When I asked why, she said it didn't look right for them to have wings. Oh, my, I just loved that! To her innocent mind angels and persons were the same, so why the wings?

One time I took a course in Renaissance Art at UCLA. I learned that one of the painters of the day decided not to paint a halo over Jesus' head which all artists were doing at that time. For not painting in the halo he had to endure much criticism. Although I cannot be certain, I believe his intention was to make Jesus look like other people. Was there not an implication here that Jesus' humanity was no different from ours, and that perhaps our lives are lived on the same level as his, including all the potential he demonstrated? This painter was most unpopular in his day, but he set a precedent for others, and later on paintings of Jesus often do not show a halo. So, in an artistic way, Jesus became interpreted in the same manner that we all are: as *Person, Man, Present Being.*

When one is ready his angelic God-consciousness expands into all that is heavenly and holy here on earth. Our divine intelligence is not just a method of tuning in the infinite; it is being involved so completely that we live an infinite experience wherever we are. Intelligence respects all religious commitments and the consecration that is given to religious feelings. Knowing that no one religion has a corner on the Truth, and accepting the omniscience of it all, we find that no denomination or sect is left out. All deal with inner-soul-searchings for higher goals. It is well to remember one

of our hymns, the words to which are written by John
Greenleaf Whittier.[122]

> O, sometimes gleams upon our sight,
> . . . th' eternal right;
> And step by step, since time began,
> We see the steady gain of man.

> For all of good the past hath had
> Remains to make our own time glad,
> Our common, daily life divine,
> And every land a Palestine.

> Hence-forth my heart shall sigh no more
> For olden time and holier shore:
> God's love and blessing, then and there,
> Are now and here and everywhere.

Some friends invited my husband and me to attend
one of their church meetings. They said they wanted
us to hear the spiritual benediction given by their minister at the close of the service. We accepted their invitation, and as the meeting was ending we were able
to understand their desire for us to have this special
experience with them. At the close of the service the
lights in the church dimmed slowly and as the benediction was spoken one could actually feel a spiritual
Oneness relating all who were present. There was a
special reverence during the silence which followed the

------

122. *Christian Science Hymnal* #239

minister's words. It gave us an enlarged understanding of the consecration of these people. We were impressed by the special beauty of their service, and we saw again how infinite are the expressions of man's religious experience.

Every religion that I know has as its basis an all-encompassing love, and as we understand the motivations of the many personal revelators we find ourselves in a glorious Oneness with them all. We rejoice in the sincerity man has within himself in exploring his own divinity, the greatness of his sacred and harmonious soul. What we are doing is extending our concept of love, knowing the full meaning of Mrs. Eddy's statement: "Divine Love always has met and always will meet every human need."[123] We do not need to ask how it is meeting it, or when, or even why it does not meet it at a special moment in time or in a special way. We accept that whatever is happening, love is taking over. This very expectancy of good underlies every correct metaphysical healing. "Jesus beheld in Science the perfect man . . ."[124] When you expect perfection you hold it in mind and you visualize it mentally in *actual existence before it is seen in form and substance!* It was in this manner Jesus' healings were performed. Similarly, a continuing need for religious organization can dissolve if that need has already been met in another way. If this happens in one's life only he may know how or why but, regardless, we rejoice with him in his divine direction. In other words we have come at last to that spiritual apprehension where

---

123. *S. & H.* 494:10-11
124. *S. & H.* 476:32 to 477:1

we let divine love alone govern man *without reservation*.

The definition of *knowledge* which you find in the *Glossary* tells us it is evidence gained from corporeal sense, that it is the origin of sin, sickness and death, and that it is the opposite of Truth. Now, thank goodness, we can relate to the higher order of knowledge because *as it* the evidences obtained from our five corporeal senses, our mortality, beliefs, and opinions, human theories, doctrines and hypotheses — all are manifestations of Mind. Why? Because our premise tells us that "All is infinite Mind and its infinite manifestation . . ."[125] This is the rock on which Mrs. Eddy based her higher concepts. With it as *your* premise you cannot be opposed to material knowledge in any form. As a matter of fact we do not recognize *any* opposite to spiritual Truth. Our work is synthesizing, combining all the elements of man's experience to bring the evidence of Truth into full view.

Let me describe a cartoon I saw recently; it is self-explanatory. We see a picture of a woman planting bulbs in her garden. A friend who is standing by watching her says, "I just couldn't plant spring-flowering bulbs this year knowing that I would be bringing them into a world of ugliness!" There is silent astonishment on the face of the woman who is placing her bulbs in the earth! It is obvious that *she* is seeing her world full of flowers even as she is planting the bulbs, while her friend sees only disappointment. Choose now how you will see your world. All of this leads me again to the wonderful world *we walk through with and as*

---

125. *S. & H.* 468:10-11

our five corporeal, knowledgeable senses, living in a divine mortality where ". . . step by step, since time began, we see the steady gain of man."

J. Bronowski says, "Man ascends by discovering the fullness of his own gifts . . . what he creates on the way are monuments to the stages in his understanding of nature and of self."[126] His book, *The Ascent of Man,* is so great a study that I leave it to you to ponder the variety of its historical references and the depth of its knowledge and wisdom. In asking the classes of students how many were familiar with this book, I have been delighted to find some who had followed the television series based on it. I recommend it to all who wish to be further enlightened about our wonderful, evolving, unfolding, expanding, creative universe.

The ascent he describes is a historical picture of man's growth in art, in science, music, architecture, religion and philosophy, but the thread and theme existing all the while is the consistent wonder, enthusiasm, and integrity of *Man.* He gives us a comprehensive list of those who have made extraordinary contributions to mankind. In our harmony of Being we experience a spiritual ascent, and in it we are gratefully identifying, relating, appreciating, harmonizing and unifying all creation as our universe, our personal, grand pantheism. We see it as the glorious infinitude of human potential in a panorama of past and present achievements. Bronowski groups his ideas beautifully, bringing them together in an orderly sequence of discernment. Most of

---

126. J. Bronowski: *The Ascent of Man.* Little, Brown and Company, Boston, Toronto, 1973, cover.

all he respects man's *imagination,* the wondrous quality
that finds its fulfillment in reaching for the stars!

Isn't it exciting that we are able to have an interest
in all of the developing sciences? You know this is a
great step in your *personal* ascent. You realize that in
it you are not accepting the limitations of what you
once thought was the history of error. Concepts of
human origin and materialistic progress you are accepting today with gratitude. The accounts of his-
torians, of natural scientists, religionists, statesmen, in-
ventors and artists are records of the material/spiritual
nature of man. We extol them freely; we rejoice in the
ever-increasing fund of knowledge that comes from
man's great imagination and which is expressed in substantial creativity as Man's concrete Being.

Someone told me that the only thing she felt missing
in Bronowski's book was the history of God! I promise
you that God, as we understand God from our work in
The Higher Order of Science, is found on every page!
The ascent of material man is synonymous with the fulfillment of spiritual man. You recognize this union as
your divinity.

What has all this to do with the harmony of your
Being? Simply this: that our soul/senses take in the
beauties of the world wherever they appear, and the
forms are infinite. Bronowski's book covers man's rising into a state of majestic greatness in every creative
path of life. Finding the challenges great, he accepts
the rewards which are so satisfying and he takes the
inevitable steps to increase his capacities through his
use of *knowledge* and *intelligence.* This is the higher
order of Man's Self-interpretation. Such an ascent
could be emphasized in the Lesson-Sermons of the

Christian Science Church, replacing the outmoded concept of "fallen man," an obsolete notion whose time
is long past. No recycling of it. Just say, "This is what
we once had within the instruction of Christian Science: *Adam and Fallen Man,* but now we move on in
the higher order of Science to *Man, Present Being,*
and I know that the time is come." *The Bridge* dis-
cusses present-day living as the living of our divinity
in the chapter entitled *Man, Present Being,* and it is
in this living that the harmony of Being is reached and
glorified.

In the definition of *Japhet* in the *Glossary,* page 589,
we find this son of Noah described as "A type of spiritual peace, flowing from the understanding that God
is the divine Principle of all existence, and that man is
His idea, the child of His care." If you feel separated
from *Japhet* by generations of history, you don't have
to because you have something marvelously in common
with him for you have this peace now, and the same
understanding of God is with you, informing you that
your divine Principle *is* your existence. The Christ consciousness of your being is the Christ child within you,
forever cared for and forever loved.

> Before me peaceful,
> Behind me peaceful,
> Under me peaceful,
> Over me peaceful,
> All around me peaceful.
>
>   Navajo Indian

Flow, flow, flow,
The current of life
is ever onward . . .

> Kobadiashi

But such is the irresistable
nature of truth, that all it
asks, and all it wants, is
the liberty of appearing.

> Thomas Paine

O wonderful, wonderful
And most wonderful, wonderful
And yet again—wonderful.

> William Shakespeare

There is always music amongst the trees in
the garden, but our hearts must be very quiet
to hear it.

> Minnie Aumonier

I'm not trying to counsel any of you to do
anything special except to dare to think, to
go with the truth, and to really love completely.

> Buckminster Fuller

And shall not loveliness be loved forever.

> Euripedes

The sun setting is no less beautiful than the
sun rising.

> Paul Green

In conclusion I wish to read a most appropriate poem written by Elena Goforth Whitehead, the same author whose poetry I have previously shared with you. As you hear it read, make it your own experience, harmonize as it.

JOY IS AN INNER SONG

The harmony of life can never cease;
Within me is contentment to be sung,
A song of spirit's beauty, love and peace,
Of deep accord with those I live among.
I blend my words with beauty and its ways
And voice the love that I personify.
I let my music be a song of praise
That peace pervades the place I occupy.
I harmonize my days as I attune
My hours to spirit, perfect at their center.
My gladness overflows as I commune
With states of grace, where only joy can enter.
Dawn gives me life renewed and hope upspringing
And, for delight, an inner song for singing.[127]

---

127. Elena Goforth Whitehead: *Attitudes*. Privately Printed, 378 Belmont Street, Oakland, California 94610, page 34.

POEMS

BIBLIOGRAPHY

Boone, J. Allen. *Kinship With All Life.* Harper & Row, Publishers, Inc., 10 East 53rd Street, New York, New York. 1954.

Bronowski, J. *The Ascent of Man.* Little, Brown and Company, Publishers, 34 Beacon Street, Boston, Mass. 1973.

Burroughs, John. *Waiting,* THE LIGHT OF DAY. Houghton Mifflin Co., Two Park Street, Boston, Mass, N.D.

Christian Science Hymnal, Hymn #239, by John Greenleaf Whittier. The Christian Science Publishing Society, Boston. 1932.

Cooper, W. Norman. *Finding Your Self.* DeVorss and Company, 1046 Princeton Drive, Marina del Rey, California. 1974.

Cousins, Norman. *The Celebration of Life: A dialogue on Immortality and Infinity.* Harper & Row, Publishers, Inc., 10 East 53rd Street, New York, N.Y. 1974.

Dorsey, John M., M.D. *Illness or Allness.* Wayne State University Press, Office of The University Professor, Detroit, Michigan. 1965.

Eddy, Mary Baker. *Science and Health with Key to the Scriptures.* Published by the Trustees under the Will of Mary Baker G. Eddy, Boston, U.S.A. 1910.
Prose Works other than Science and Health. Published by the Trustees under the Will of Mary Baker G. Eddy, Boston, U.S.A. 1925.
Christian Science Hymnal. Mother's Evening Prayer, Hymn #207. 1932.

Eliot, T. S. *Little Gidding,* FOUR QUARTETS. Published by Harcourt Brace Jovanovich, Inc., New York, N.Y.— also Faber and Faber. Ltd., London. N.D.

Glasser, William, M.D. *Reality Therapy: A New Approach To Psychiatry,* Harper & Row, Publishers, Inc., 10 East 53rd Street, New York, N.Y. 1965.

153

Harris, Thomas A. M.D. *I'M OK—YOU'RE OK*. Harper & Row, Publishers, Inc., 10 East 53rd Street, New York, N.Y. 1963.

Judah, J. Stillson. *The History and Philosophy of The Metaphysical Movements in America*. The Westminster Press, Philadelphia, Pennsylvania, copyright MCMLXVII.

Maharishi Mahesh Yogi. *The Science of Being and Art of Living*. International SRM Publications. 1966. National Center for The Transcendental Meditation Program, 17310 Sunset Boulevard, Pacific Palisades, California 90272.

McDaniel, James. *Martin Luther: A Magnet For All Christians*. Publishers, Reader's Digest, Pleasantville, New York. 1968.

Moore, Irene S. *The Bridge*. Published by DeVorss & Co., 1046 Princeton Drive, Marina del Rey, California. 1971. *Identity*. Published by DeVorss & Co., 1046 Princeton Drive, Marina del Rey, California. 1974.

Nureyev, Rudolph. *Nureyev: an autobiography*. Publishers, E. P. Dutton & Co., Inc., 201 Park Avenue South, New York, N.Y. 1963.

Rubinstein, Arthur. *My Young Years*. Published by Alfred A. Knopf. Inc., 201 East 50th Street, New York, N.Y. 1973.

Rush, Rozella. *Mortal/Immortal Now*. INSIGHTS. Publishing office 2217 Clark Building, Pittsburgh, Pa. 1975.

Steinbeck, John. *Steinbeck: A Life In Letters*. Edited by Elaine Steinbeck and Robert Wallsten. The Viking Press, 625 Madison Avenue, New York, N.Y. 1975.

Strong, Mary (Editor). *Letters of The Scattered Brotherhood*. Harper & Row, Publishers, Inc., New York, N.Y. 1948.

Studdert-Kennedy, Hugh A. *Christian Science and Organized Religion*. The Farallon Press, Los Gatos, California. 1947.

Whitehead, Elena Goforth. *Attitudes*. Privately Printed. 378 Belmont Street, Oakland, California. 1973.

Whitman, Howard. *Points to Ponder*. Reader's Digest, August 1974. The Register and Tribune Syndicate, Inc., 715 Locust Street, Des Moines, Iowa 50304.